All Scripture references taken from the KJV of the Holy Bible, unless otherwise indicated.

THRONES: It's Not A Game

Who Rules, Who Rebels & Why It Matters

by Dr. Marlene Miles

Freshwater Press 2026

ISBN: 978-1-971933-36-8

Paperback Version

I0835102

Table of Contents

THRONES: It's Not A Game

Who Rules, Who Rebels & Why It Matters

by Dr. Marlene Miles

And every creature which is in heaven, and on the earth, and under the earth, and such as are in the sea, and all that are in them, heard I saying, Blessing, and honour, and glory, and power, be unto him that sitteth upon the throne, and unto the Lamb for ever and ever.

Revelation 5:13

Psalm 93

The Lord reigneth, he is clothed with majesty; the Lord is clothed with strength, wherewith he hath girded himself: the world also is stablished, that it cannot be moved.

Thy throne is established of old: thou art from everlasting.

The floods have lifted up, O Lord, the floods have lifted up their voice; the floods lift up their waves.

The Lord on high is mightier than the noise of many waters, yea, than the mighty waves of the sea.

Thy testimonies are very sure: holiness becometh thine house, O Lord, for ever.

The Lord reigneth.

The psalm begins with a declaration, not a request. "The Lord reigneth…" God *will* reign if people acknowledge Him or not; that is a **present and settled reality**. God's kingship is already established.

Human recognition does not create it — it **confesses** it.

Clothed with majesty… clothed with strength. This is describing royal authority. Kings in the ancient world wore robes, armor, or ceremonial garments that symbolized power. The psalmist uses that imagery to say that God's rule is wrapped in majesty and strength. His authority is not fragile.

The world also is established, that it cannot be moved. This connects God's throne to cosmic stability. Because God reigns, Creation itself is held in order. The throne is not merely symbolic. It is the foundation of reality.

Thy throne is established of old. This is one of the strongest statements in Scripture about God's throne. "Thy throne is established of old: thou art from everlasting" means the throne did not begin in Time. It was not created by events in history. It existed before Creation.

God's rule is **eternal**, not reactive.

The LORD hath prepared his throne in the heavens;
and his kingdom ruleth over all. (Psalms 103:19)

The floods and the waves of Verses 3–4 introduce chaos imagery. In ancient Hebrew poetry, floods and roaring seas often represent chaos, disorder, or threatening powers. The world can appear turbulent: "The floods have lifted up their voice…" But God immediately answers it. "The Lord on high is mightier…"

So even though chaos rises, God's throne remains higher.

The psalm ends not with fear, but with certainty, *Thy testimonies are very sure: holiness becometh thine house.* God's throne is stable, His Word is reliable and His house is holy. Rule and righteousness go together.

This psalm describes the throne of God in three dimensions:

1. **Eternal** – established "of old."
2. **Cosmic** – the world stands because of it.
3. **Moral** – holiness belongs in God's House.

The throne is not just authority, it is also **the source of order, truth, and holiness**. Because God's Throne is eternal, the world is stable even when chaos roars.

Psalm 93 sits inside a small cluster of psalms often called the enthronement psalms, 93–99, and they all circle around one central declaration: The Lord reigns. They don't enthrone God in the sense of making Him king; they announce and celebrate the throne that already exists.

The Enthronement Psalms (Psalm 93–99),

Psalm 93 — The Throne Is Eternal -Theme: God's throne is established before creation and cannot be shaken. The Lord reigns. His throne is from everlasting. Chaos (the floods) cannot overthrow Him. It establishes the foundation of the throne.

Psalm 94 — The Judge of the Earth. After establishing the throne, what does the King do? Psalm 94 answers: He judges injustice. God is called:

O Lord God, to whom vengeance belongeth.

This psalm shows the throne as **judicial authority**. The king defends the oppressed and calls wicked rulers to account.

Psalm 95 — The Call to Worship the King. This psalm invites people to respond to God's kingship.

O come, let us worship and bow down: let us kneel before the Lord our maker.

The Throne now moves from cosmic reality to human response. Then the psalm ends with a warning. Recognition of the throne requires obedience.

Today if you hear his voice, harden not your heart…

Psalm 96 — The King Over All Nation. God's reign is not limited to Israel. This psalm announces that the Lord reigns over the whole Earth, not just one people group. The Throne becomes global.

Declare his glory among the heathen, his wonders among all people.

Psalm 97 — The King Appears.

Clouds and darkness are round about him: righteousness and judgment are the habitation of his throne.

This psalm describes the manifestation of God's rule. Mountains melt. Earth trembles. This is throne language in motion.

Psalm 98 — The King Has Won

Now the focus shifts to **victory**.

"The Lord hath made known his salvation…"

This psalm celebrates what God has **done in history**.

The throne is not only eternal; it **acts to save**.

Psalm 99 — The Holy King.

The final psalm of this grouping returns to the Throne itself.

The Lord reigneth; let the people tremble: he sitteth between the cherubims.

Now we see the Throne, holiness, reverence and worship. The psalm ends with the refrain:

Exalt the Lord our God… for he is holy.

The last word of the enthronement psalms is **holiness**.

These psalms form a kind of progression:

1. **Psalm 93** — The throne exists eternally.
2. **Psalm 94** — The king judges injustice.
3. **Psalm 95** — People are called to worship.
4. **Psalm 96** — The king reigns over all nations.
5. **Psalm 97** — The king appears in power.
6. **Psalm 98** — The king brings salvation.
7. **Psalm 99** — The king is holy.

It moves from cosmic throne to human response to global reign to holiness. The Throne of God is not just a doctrine. It affects Creation, Justice, worship, nations, salvation, and holiness. God's Throne is the center of everything.

Justice and judgment are the habitation of thy throne: mercy and truth shall go before thy face.
(Psalms 89:14)

Some scholars believe these psalms may have been used during a temple festival celebrating the kingship of God. And the way they are arranged is not random. It's almost like a liturgical proclamation of the throne.

Scholars often call Psalms 93–99 the "YHWH-Malak psalms" (from the Hebrew phrase meaning "The LORD reigns"). The idea is that these psalms may have been sung in the temple during a festival celebrating God as the true king of Israel and of the world.

This does not mean God was being made king at that moment. It means the community was publicly proclaiming and celebrating the kingship that already existed.

The Temple was the Place of the Throne. In Israel's theology, the temple symbolized the earthly focal point of God's rule.

He sitteth between the cherubim. (Psalm 99)

That refers to the Ark of the Covenant inside the Holy of Holies, where two cherubim faced each other over the Mercy Seat.

The ark was not literally God's throne, but it symbolized His governing presence among His people. The temple worship was like a public acknowledgment of Heaven's Throne.

The festival proclamation pattern was such that if these psalms were used in a festival, the sequence makes sense as a proclamation of the king.

It may have sounded something like this:

1. Psalm 93 – Declaration: *The Lord reigns.*
2. Psalm 95 – Invitation: *Come worship the king.*
3. Psalm 96 – Announcement: *Tell the nations the king reigns.*
4. Psalm 97 – Manifestation: *The king appears in power.*
5. Psalm 98 – Celebration: *The king has brought salvation.*
6. Psalm 99 – Reverence: *The king is holy.*

It moves from proclamation to worship to the global announcement, to reverence and awe, to celebration, and then to holiness. That progression feels very much like a coronation liturgy, except the king is God Himself.

Israel lived in a world where every nation had a visible king, and powerful empires ruled the Earth. By singing "The Lord reigns," Israel was declaring that even if earthly kingdoms dominate the moment, the ultimate throne belongs to God. It was both worship and theological resistance.

This idea flows forward into the New Testament. When the Kingdom of God is announced, it is essentially saying that the true King is acting and establishing His rule.

So, the enthronement psalms become part of the larger Biblical story of God's kingship over Creation and history.

God reigneth over the heathen: God sitteth upon the throne of his holiness. (Psalms 47:8)

WHAT IS A THRONE?

A physical throne is a chair. A throne in the natural has upholstery, ornamentation, position, and elevation for spectacle. It is a royal chair or seat of dignity. It is often ornate, made with inlays of wood, gold and other expensive substances. It is elevated so the steps are part of the ornamentation.

It is a royal seat, a chair of state. The *throne* is sometimes an elegant chair richly decorated with sculpture and gilding, raised a step above the floor, and covered with a canopy.

Throne is also described as the seat of a bishop. In Scripture, it represents or seats sovereign power and dignity. Another definition of a throne is Angels (Colossians 1:16). And it is also the place where God peculiarly manifests His power and glory.

This book is not about that.

Spiritually speaking--, yes, we are speaking of spiritual thrones. A throne is t**he seat of ultimate governing authority from which decree, judgment, and jurisdiction proceed.**

For there are set thrones of judgment, the thrones of the house of David. (Psalm 122:5)

A throne represents the right to rule, the power to define boundaries. It represents the authority to issue binding decrees. From it proceeds the final word in a given jurisdiction. It is the source from which order is enforced. A throne is not about elegance and comfort as much as it is about command.

A throne is not identical to a covenant, but a throne is sustained by covenants. A throne is the seat of rule; covenants are the agreements that stabilize that rule.

Thrones require covenant loyalty. In the ancient world, a king did not rule by force alone. His throne depended on covenantal relationships with his people, his nobles, allied rulers, and sometimes with God depending on if he was an evil king or a Godly one. If those covenants broke down, the throne became unstable.

For example, when Israel rejected God's covenant, the kingdom itself collapsed (2 Kings 17). The throne failed because the covenant foundation failed.

God's Throne itself is described as being upheld by covenant qualities. Psalm language says, Righteousness and justice are the foundation of Your throne. (Psalms 89:14)

Those qualities are covenantal attributes. God rules through faithfulness, Justice and Mercy. His

Throne is stable because **His covenant faithfulness never fails**.

3. The Throne of David Is Explicitly Covenant-Based. The throne of David exists because of a **covenant promise**.

> Your house and your kingdom shall endure forever before me; your throne shall be established forever. (2 Samuel 7:16)

That throne exists because of covenant, not just political power. Even when the monarchy collapsed, the covenant promise remained.

Thrones collapse when covenants collapse. Many Biblical throne conflicts happen when covenant loyalty breaks. For example, Saul loses his throne because of disobedience. Israel's kings fall because they abandon the covenant. Empires collapse when alliances and loyalties dissolve. So, the throne itself sits on a web of covenant relationships.

A throne is the seat of authority, but it rests upon covenants. Covenants create the loyalties that make a throne stable. Without covenant, authority becomes tyranny, loyalty disappears, and the throne collapses.

> But when his heart was lifted up, and his mind hardened in pride, he was deposed from his kingly throne, and they took his glory from him. (Daniel 5:20)

The Kingdom of God operates on the New Covenant established through Christ (Luke 22:20).

That covenant creates the loyalty and relationship that allows Believers to participate in the Kingdom. So even in the New Testament, authority and covenant remain connected.

A throne is the seat of authority sustained by covenants of loyalty.

In Scripture, when a throne appears, several realities are implied:

1. **Jurisdiction** — There is a defined realm under rule.
2. **Legitimacy** — The ruler possesses recognized authority.
3. **Decree** — What is spoken from the throne carries binding force.
4. **Accountability** — Lesser authorities answer upward.
5. **Finality** — Appeals terminate at the throne.

That is why heavenly scenes always place the throne at the center. It's not so much that God needs a seat, but because rule must be seen as structured.

A throne only exists in relation to subjects. Authority requires recognition. This is why rebellion is described as throne conflict — not because the throne disappears, but because allegiance shifts.

A throne can be rejected, but it cannot be erased. A throne can be occupied, vacated, transferred, and fulfilled. But the authority it represents ultimately belongs to the Highest --, the Throne of God.

The real conflict in history is not simply who sits on a throne, but whether the throne itself is acknowledged. Kings may fall. Nations may vanish. But the idea of rightful authority — the Throne itself — continues under the sovereignty of God.

Influence persuades. A throne governs. Influence suggests. A throne decrees. Influence invites. A throne commands. Counterfeit thrones often begin as influence. They become thrones when allegiance stabilizes them.

If we misunderstand a throne as a symbol of prestige, we will miss the seriousness of throne conflict. But if we understand it as the seat of ultimate jurisdiction, then we recognize several things. The wilderness was about jurisdiction. The Cross was about jurisdiction. Word curses are about jurisdiction. The heart is about jurisdiction.

Every conflict in Scripture is ultimately a conflict of thrones — because every conflict is about who has the final word.

THRONES MATTER

The Bible is not primarily a book about feelings. It is a book about authority. From Genesis to Revelation, Scripture is concerned with one central question: Who has the right to rule?

Creation itself begins with government. Light is separated from darkness. Waters are bounded. Time is ordered. Human beings are given dominion.

Authority is not an afterthought in Scripture — it is the framework through which everything else is understood. Yet modern Believers often approach the Bible as though it were a moral handbook, a comfort manual, a collection of inspirational sayings. In doing so, we miss its central architecture. The Bible is a constitutional document of the Kingdom of God.

It tells us who reigns, how rebellion began, how authority was challenged, how counterfeit thrones were erected, how Christ confronted them, and where rule must ultimately be settled.

Every conflict in Scripture is a throne conflict.

Every temptation is an authority test.

Every covenant is a transfer of allegiance.

Every act of obedience either preserves or shifts jurisdiction.

There is no neutral ground.

The human heart has a throne.

Heaven has an Eternal Throne. Nations have delegated thrones.

Darkness attempts to establish thrones; those are counterfeit thrones.

History moves toward the public revelation of the One whose Throne cannot be shaken.

This book will examine thrones as they function in Scripture as seats of government. They are positions of jurisdiction. They are centers of decree and sources of law. They are structures of allegiance.

We will look first at the Eternal Throne — the authority that existed before Lucifer's rebellion. Then this book will look at created thrones. After that, ranks and dominions operating under command. Then we will examine usurped and counterfeit thrones, which are the structures of darkness that mimic Godly rule. Then we will look at the confrontation of those thrones in Christ.

Finally, we will arrive at the most consequential throne of all: the throne of the human heart. Because the greatest battleground for the souls of men is the human heart.

Salvation is not merely forgiveness. It is allegiance. It is governmental transfer.

This book does not promote fear of darkness, it's powers, principalities or thrones, but it is a call to the Eternal Throne which has all power. All power belongs to God.

When authority is understood, confusion loses power. When jurisdiction is recognized, intimidation weakens. When the rightful King is seen, rival thrones collapse. There is only one Throne that does not depend on suggestion, force, manipulation, or fear. It is the Eternal Throne of God, and it existed before Creation, and it remained after Resurrection. It cannot be eclipsed or collapsed; it will last forever and ever. Amen.

Every other throne will eventually answer to it.

We will see how every conflict in Scripture is ultimately a conflict of thrones. Eden was a conflict of thrones. The Wilderness was a conflict of thrones. The Cross was a conflict of thrones. Word curses, false prophecy, and idolatry are all conflicts of thrones. Fear is a conflict of thrones. The human heart is a conflict of thrones, and often daily.

BEFORE CREATION: THE THRONE THAT WAS

Before there was light, there was rule. Before there were Angels, there was authority. Before there was rebellion, there was a Throne. Scripture does not begin by introducing God as an idea; it introduces Him as Sovereign.

"In the beginning, God…" God did not *become* King. He was already. There was absolute authority before opposition. God's Throne was not established in response to rebellion. It did not form because Lucifer fell. It did not solidify because humanity sinned. It was not strengthened by the Cross. It existed before all of it. Authority did not arise from conflict. Conflict arose from authority.

If authority were reactive, then rebellion would shape it. If God's rule were defensive, then opposition would refine it. Scripture never presents God as consolidating power. His Throne is described as **established**, eternal, unshaken and from everlasting. This Throne that predates Creation cannot be threatened by it or any part of it.

When Scripture speaks of a throne, it is not describing ornamentation. A throne represents jurisdiction, decree, final word, law, governance, and supremacy. A spiritual throne is the seat from which reality is ordered. When Genesis opens, the ordering of Creation flows from an already-settled authority. Light separates because Someone commands it. Waters divide because Someone speaks boundary. Time begins because Someone defines it. That Someone is Jehovah God. Creation does not negotiate; it responds.

Heaven is not a democracy; it is a theocracy. Many assume power must be justified by consensus. Heaven does not function by vote; it functions by recognition. Worship in Scripture is not flattery; it is agreement with rightful rule. The heavenly host does not strengthen God by praise. They acknowledge what is already true.

> And the four and twenty elders and the four beasts fell down and worshipped God that sat on the throne, saying, Amen; Alleluia. (Revelation 19:4)

This is why rebellion in Heaven was not a political movement; it was a Throne challenge. It failed not because it lacked strategy, but because it lacked origin.

Only one Throne is uncreated. Everything else is derivative. All other authority in existence is delegated. Angels derive authority. Humanity derives authority. Nations derive authority. Spiritual ranks derive authority. None originate it. That means no other throne in Creation is self-sustaining.

Remove the Source, and the seat collapses. This is why Scripture consistently distinguishes between the Throne of God and lesser thrones, dominions, principalities, and powers. The first is eternal. The rest are assigned.

We are not told much about the state of Heaven before rebellion. That silence and stillness is instructive. Scripture does not dramatize the pre-fall cosmos. It assumes order, harmony, alignment. There was no tension, no rival decree, no second voice.

Authority was uncontested not because it was fragile, but because it was absolute. Rebellion does not introduce authority into the universe. It introduces fracture.

We must understand the origin of God's Throne to properly interpret every conflict that follows. If we imagine God reacting, we will imagine Him threatened. If we imagine Him consolidating power, we will imagine Him insecure. His Throne predates every rival voice; therefore, every later conflict is not about survival, but about revelation. There was a Throne before there was opposition, and that Throne has never been vacated.

THE THRONE IN HEAVEN

Scripture does not leave the Throne of God abstract; it reveals it.

When the prophet **Isaiah** is granted vision, he does not first describe angels, or clouds, or light. He writes:

I saw the Lord sitting upon a throne, high and lifted up; and the train of His robe filled the temple.

The throne is elevated. Not to inspire awe alone — but to signify supremacy. The posture is seated. God is not pacing. He is not striving. He is not contending for position. He is enthroned.

When **Daniel** records his vision, the imagery becomes even more explicit, with courtroom language. The Throne is a judicial seat.

The thrones were set in place, and the Ancient of Days took His seat… His throne was fiery flames; its wheels were burning fire.

Thrones are "set in place." Judgment is seated. Books are opened. Decrees proceed. Heaven is ordered government. The Ancient of Days does not ascend to His throne in Daniel's vision. He takes His seat. It was His already.

Worship recognizes rule. In Revelation, John is caught up. He writes,

> Immediately I was in the Spirit; and behold, a throne stood in heaven, with One seated on the throne.

A throne *stood.* Stable. Established. Around it elders, living creatures, lightning and thunder, a sea like crystal, and a scroll sealed with seven seals.

And what do the elders do?

> They fall down before Him who sits on the throne… saying, 'You are worthy, O Lord, to receive glory and honor and power.'

Worship is not performance. It is recognition. Heaven does not create God's authority by praise. It acknowledges what is already incontestable.

Revelation also introduces a distinction that must not be missed. There is the Throne and thrones. Around the Throne, twenty-four elders sit on their own thrones, but their thrones are positioned, derived; this is delegated authority.

The Elders remove their crowns and cast them before the Central Seat of authority. This is a visual theology of delegated authority. Every lesser throne must eventually answer to the Greater One. No created seat is self-sustaining.

This is why the Lamb's appearance in Revelation 5 is seismic. The scroll cannot be opened. Authority cannot proceed. History pauses. Then the Lamb appears, and takes the scroll from the right hand of Him who sits on the Throne.

The Son operates in perfect alignment with the Father's Throne, not as rival or replacement; but as authorized executor.

and the government shall be upon his shoulder: and his name shall be called Wonderful, Counsellor, The mighty God, The everlasting Father, The Prince of Peace. (Isaiah 9:6b)

Heaven is structured, not chaotic. Modern spirituality often imagines Heaven as vaporous light and endless song. Scripture presents something more formidable. There is the Central, Eternal Throne and there are thrones, ranks, decrees, seals, books, elders, and witnesses.

Authority is layered, not competitive — but ordered. The Throne at the center does not strain to remain central. Everything else orbits it. This Throne is unshaken and unshakeable. The Psalms repeatedly anchor this reality:

The Lord has established His throne in the heavens, and His kingdom rules over all.

Established, not aspiring. It is not fragile, or awaiting endorsement. It <u>**is**</u>. If the Heavenly Throne were unstable, then every earthly conflict becomes existential. The Throne of God is settled, therefore rebellion is not a threat to God.

It is a threat to the rebel.

Before we examine counterfeit thrones, we must see the real one clearly. Before we speak of usurpation, we must see origin. Before we speak of spiritual warfare, we must understand jurisdiction. Heaven does not react; it rules.

The Throne of God is not an emergency seat. It is the axis around which all other authority turns. Nothing in Creation has ever occupied it by accident.

WHAT HAPPENS AT A THRONE

1. Decrees Are Issued

A throne is where laws and commands originate.

Kings speak from the throne, and their words become binding orders. In the Bible this shows up when rulers issue decrees that affect whole nations. The throne is therefore the source of authority that sets direction for a realm.

2. Judgments Are Rendered.

Thrones are places of justice. People bring disputes, accusations, or appeals to the throne because the king (or judge) has the final authority to decide what is right. That is why Scripture often describes God's throne with words like righteousness and justice. The throne is the highest court.

Let us therefore come boldly unto the throne of grace, that we may obtain mercy, and find grace to help in time of need. (Hebrews 4:16)

3. Petitions Are Presented

Subjects come before a throne to ask for something. They may seek Mercy, protection, favor, provision, or intervention. A well-known Biblical example is when Esther approaches Ahasuerus to plead for her people in Esther.

The throne is where requests are heard and answered.

4. Allegiance Is Declared

People come to a throne to acknowledge the ruler's authority.

This may include bowing, presenting tribute, or pledging loyalty. In other words, a throne is where political and covenant allegiance becomes visible.

5. Rewards Are Granted

Kings often use the throne to honor and elevate others. From the throne a ruler may grant land, give titles, appoint officials, and reward service.

In the Biblical narrative this happens when faithful servants are promoted or honored.

6. Authority Is Delegated

The throne is also where positions of authority are assigned. Officials, governors, and judges receive their roles from the king's authority. The throne therefore becomes the center of government, from which other authorities flow.

7. **Presence Is Recognized –**

Finally, the throne represents the ruler's presence. Even when the king is not speaking, the throne signals: The ruler is here. Authority resides here. That is why throne rooms were designed to be impressive, to visually reinforced the reality of rule.

People approach a throne because it is the place where ultimate authority resides. They go there when they need something that only the highest authority can provide, such as Justice and Mercy. From this authority we receive permission, protection, recognition, decisions, rulings, and decrees.

People go to a throne because that is where the final word is spoken.

When the Bible speaks about approaching God's throne, it uses this same idea. The throne represents the place where justice is established, Mercy is given, authority is exercised, and Creation is governed. It is the center of rule.

A throne is where laws are declared. judgments are made. petitions are heard. loyalty is affirmed. rewards are granted. authority is delegated. the ruler's presence is recognized. People go to a throne because it is the place of final decision.

The throne and the scepter. If you sit on a throne, you have a crown. Where is your crown? If you sit on a throne you judge. You rule. You speak. You proclaim and you make decrees. The seat of the high priest is a throne. We are all seated in Heavenly places with Christ Jesus.

The throne represents the seat of authority. The crown represents recognized honor. The scepter represents the active exercise of rule. A king seated on a throne but without a scepter possesses authority but does not yet exercise it.

When the scepter is raised, authority becomes law, judgment, or Mercy. The scepter is the difference between having authority and exercising authority.

THE PRIMARY FUNCTIONS OF GOD'S THRONE IN SCRIPTURE

Judgment is the most frequent throne activity. The throne is repeatedly described as a seat of judgment. From there God evaluates, decides, and renders justice. Examples appear throughout Psalms, Daniel, and Revelation, where the throne is the place where books are opened and verdicts are issued.

This is why phrases like "righteousness and justice are the foundation of your throne" appear repeatedly.

The Throne is fundamentally a judicial seat.

The throne is also the place of governance over creation. From the Throne, God establishes order, directs history, rules nations, and sustains Creation. His rule is Sovereign. This is what Psalm 93 expresses when it says the world is established and cannot be moved. His Throne is the center of cosmic government.

The New Testament highlights another function: Mercy. In Hebrews 4, believers are invited to approach the Throne of Grace.

That does not mean the throne changed into a different throne. It means the same throne of authority is approached through Christ as a place where Mercy is given instead of condemnation. The throne is also where forgiveness and help are dispensed.

Worship - Another major activity around God's throne is worship. Heavenly beings continually acknowledge the authority of the One seated there.

In Revelation 4, the elders cast their crowns before the throne and declare God worthy. This shows the Throne as the center of recognition and reverence.

God's Throne is also the source of Divine decree. From that seat God's word goes forth and shapes reality. When God speaks, events unfold accordingly. In prophetic visions, decisions about kingdoms, nations, and future events are issued from the Throne. So, the Throne is the origin of authoritative pronouncements.

Ranking the most common Throne functions in Scripture, the pattern looks like this: Judgment, Rule / governance, Worship around the throne, Mercy and help, and Divine decrees. Together these form the Biblical picture of the Throne of God.

When people approach a throne in Scripture, they are usually coming for one of four things: Justice (a decision or verdict), Mercy (forgiveness or help),

Authority (permission or decree), and Recognition to honor the king.

A throne is where ultimate authority speaks, justice is decided, mercy is granted, and allegiance is declared: it combines government, justice, mercy, and worship in one place.

The Bible shows a pattern: whenever a power tries to establish a throne independent of God, it eventually collapses.

1. The Throne of God vs. Babylon's Throne. Babylon becomes the Bible's most famous symbol of counterfeit rule. In Isaiah 14, a ruler of Babylon says:

"I will ascend… I will exalt my throne… I will be like the Most High."

Babylon represents the attempt to create a self-exalting throne, an authority that does not acknowledge God. But the prophecy ends with Babylon being cast down. The contrast is clear: God's throne is eternal. Babylon's throne is temporary.

2. The Throne of God vs. Pharaoh's Throne

In the Exodus story, Pharaoh sits on the most powerful throne in the world at that time. Pharaoh essentially claims divine authority. Egyptian kings were often treated as *gods*. The confrontation with Moses shows something important: Pharaoh's throne looks powerful, but it is not ultimate. The plagues demonstrate that the throne of Egypt cannot withstand the authority of God.

3. The Throne of God vs. Idolatrous Thrones

Many ancient cultures built literal thrones for their *gods* in temples. The prophets repeatedly say those thrones are empty. For example, in Jeremiah, idols are described as objects that cannot speak, move, or act.

So, these thrones represent imagined authority. They mimic kingship without possessing it.

4. The Throne of God vs. Satan's Throne. The New Testament briefly refers to "Satan's throne" in Revelation 2:13. This suggests a center of influence where opposition to God is concentrated. Scripture never describes Satan's throne as eternal; it is always limited and temporary.

5. The Throne of God vs. Human Self-Enthronement. Another counterfeit throne appears whenever humans try to rule without God. The Tower of Babel is a good example. People attempt to build a structure reaching Heaven — essentially establishing their own greatness and unity apart from God.

God disrupts the project, showing that human ambition cannot create a true throne. The Pattern repeatedly across Scripture. A power establishes a throne. It claims authority independent of God. It appears strong for a time. Eventually it falls.

Meanwhile, God's Throne remains unchanged.

So, the conflict in Scripture is not even between equal thrones. It is between the Eternal Throne of God and temporary thrones built by rebellion. One is permanent. The others are passing. Every throne that refuses the authority of God eventually collapses, because only one throne is eternal.

And this leads to something fascinating that fits perfectly with the image of the crowns at the base of the throne. In Revelation 4, the elders cast their crowns before the throne. That's the opposite of Babylon. Instead of trying to elevate their throne, they lay their authority down before the true King.

GOD'S THRONE – DAVID'S THRONE

(For thus saith the LORD; David shall never want a man to sit upon the throne of the house of Israel; (Jeremiah 33:17)

The throne of David is one of the most important bridges in the whole Bible between earthly kingship and God's eternal throne. It explains how the Bible moves from God reigning in heaven to the Messiah ruling on earth.

God Is the Original King. Before Israel ever had human kings, God was already their ruler. When Israel asks for a king in 1 Samuel 8, God tells the prophet Samuel:

They have not rejected thee, but they have rejected me, that I should not reign over them.

It shows that Israel already had a king: God Himself. So, the throne of Israel was originally God's Throne.

David's throne is established by covenant. Later, God chooses David and makes a covenant with him in 2 Samuel 7. God promises David's house will endure. His kingdom will be established. His throne will last forever.

This promise creates the idea of the Davidic throne. But David's throne is never meant to replace God's throne. It is meant to represent God's rule on earth.

The King of Israel sits on the Lord's Throne, one passage makes this relationship very clear. When Solomon becomes king.

Then Solomon sat on the throne of the Lord as king.
(1 Chronicles 29:23)

That phrase is remarkable. It does not say Solomon sat on his own throne. It says he sat on the throne of the Lord. In other words, the king of Israel ruled as God's representative. The earthly throne reflected the Heavenly Throne.

After Solomon, many human kings of Israel and Judah failed. Some became corrupt, idolatrous, or unjust. The throne of David continues, but it becomes unstable. Eventually the kingdom collapses and the people are exiled. At that moment it appears that the Davidic throne has ended. But the prophets say the promise is not finished.

The Prophets promise a future king. Prophets like Isaiah and Jeremiah say a future descendant of David will restore the throne.

Of the increase of his government and peace there shall be no end, upon the throne of David. (Isaiah 9)

This future ruler will bring justice and righteousness forever. The throne of David becomes a Messianic promise.

The New Testament identifies Jesus Christ as that promised king. When the angel speaks to Mary in Luke 1, he says:

> The Lord God shall give unto him the throne of his father David.

So, Jesus is presented as heir of David, rightful king, and fulfillment of the covenant. But His kingship goes beyond Israel.

The Throne of David Meets the Throne of God. In the New Testament, the story reaches its climax. Jesus rises from the dead and is exalted to heaven. He is described as seated at the Right Hand of God, sharing Divine authority.

This is where the lines converge: God's Throne, David's throne, and the Messiah's rule. The earthly promise and the Heavenly Throne come together in Christ.

The Bible's throne story moves like this: God reigns as King. David's throne represents God's rule on Earth. Human kings fail. A future king is promised. Jesus fulfills the promise and reigns forever.

So, the throne of David is not separate from God's Throne. It is the earthly expression of it, fulfilled ultimately in thc Messiah. The throne of David was never meant to replace God's Throne; it was meant to reflect it until the true King came.

Then I will establish the throne of thy kingdom upon
Israel for ever, as I promised to David thy father,
saying, There shall not fail thee a man upon the
throne of Israel. (1 Kings 9:5)

CROWNS CAST DOWN

Daniel's vision is one of the earliest places this appears is in Daniel 7. Daniel sees a heavenly court scene where thrones are set in place. The "Ancient of Days" sits in judgment. Also, the Son of Man receives dominion.

> I beheld till the thrones were cast down, and the Ancient of days did sit, whose garment was white as snow, and the hair of his head like the pure wool; his throne was like the fiery flame, and his wheels as burning fire. (Daniel 7:9)

Then something surprising happens. The vision says the kingdom will be given to "the saints of the Most High."

In other words: The rule of the Messiah will eventually be shared with His people. Not independent rule — but participation in His kingdom.

Jesus speaks about future thrones later on. Jesus Christ tells His Disciples something remarkable. In Matthew 19, He says the apostles will sit on twelve thrones, judging the twelve tribes of Israel. This shows two things: authority can be delegated; thrones can be shared under a Greater Throne. The Disciples are not replacing Christ's authority. They are participating in it.

Believers will reign with Christ. This theme appears again in Revelation 20, where those who belong to Christ are described as reigning with Him. The language suggests participation in the Kingdom, shared governance under Christ, and restoration of humanity's intended role in creation.

Remember, humanity was originally given dominion in Genesis. The New Testament shows that purpose restored through Christ. Another powerful statement appears in Revelation 3 where Jesus makes a promise to the Faithful.

To the one who overcomes, I will grant to sit with me on my throne, as I also overcame and sat down with my Father on His throne.

Notice the pattern: the Father's Throne, Christ seated with the Father, then Believers seated with Christ. Authority flows downward through relationship and victory.

Scripture never suggests that Believers become independent rulers equal to God. The structure always remains God's Eternal Throne, Christ reigning as King, and His people participating in His rule.

So, any future thrones are always derivative, not sovereign. They exist because of the Central Throne, not apart from it.

If we step back, the throne story across the Bible looks like this:

1. God reigns as king over Creation.
2. Humanity is given delegated dominion.
3. That authority is corrupted by rebellion.
4. God establishes the throne of David.
5. The Messiah fulfills that throne.
6. Christ reigns forever.
7. His people share in His rule.

The throne theme runs from Genesis to David, to Messiah, to Kingdom. God alone possesses the Eternal Throne, but through Christ He invites redeemed humanity to participate in His Kingdom. The crowns laid before the throne in Revelation 4 show something profound: Even those who reign with Christ recognize that all authority ultimately belongs to God. They do not cling to their crowns. They place them before the Throne.

Satan's original rebellion in Isaiah 14 is described in throne language. It was the first attempted coup against God's Throne in the Biblical narrative.

"I will ascend into heaven,
I will exalt **my throne** above the stars of God;
I will sit also upon the mount of the congregation…
I will ascend above the heights of the clouds;
I will be like the Most High." (Isaiah 14)

The ambition is not merely power. It is **to sit where God sits**. The rebellion is fundamentally about **authority and position**.

The passage contains five declarations of self-exaltation; they are the five "I will" statements.

1. **"I will ascend into heaven."** – reaching for a higher realm of authority.
2. **"I will exalt my throne."** – establishing an independent seat of rule.
3. **"I will sit on the mount of assembly."** – taking a place in the Divine Council.
4. **"I will ascend above the clouds."** – rising above all visible creation.
5. **"I will be like the Most High."** – the ultimate claim to Divine status.

Each *I will* moves closer to usurping God's Throne.

Rebellion in Scripture is not just moral failure, it is also a challenge to rightful authority. The problem is not simply wrongdoing. The problem is self-enthronement. That theme appears again and again in the Bible: Babylon's pride, Pharaoh's defiance, human rulers who claim Divine authority. All of them reflect the same pattern: attempting to rule apart from God's Throne.

The outcome of the attempt is failure. The prophecy immediately reverses the ambition: "Yet thou shalt be brought down to the pit." The one who tried to ascend is cast down. That reversal appears throughout Scripture: self-exalting thrones collapse.

The Bible repeatedly contrasts two directions: Self-exaltation. “I will ascend.” “I will exalt my throne.”

Submission is seen in crowns laid before the Throne of God, bowing before the King, acknowledging God’s rule. The first path leads downward. The second leads to participation in God’s Kingdom.

There is one Eternal Throne, and every other authority must either align with it or eventually fall.

HIERARCHY OF GOD

We serve a God of order; there is structure in the Kingdom of Heaven, and it is so good that the devil has tried to copy it. Here on Earth, we endeavor to have order, structure and hierarchy as well. When that gets perverted, it turns into prejudice, racism, discrimination, misogyny, sexism, ageism, and caste systems, which all lead to more disorder.

There is no perversion in God, so if you see any hatred and chaos, it is the dark kingdom's system of trying to achieve hierarchy. It is man's convoluted way of asking, *Which one is better than the other? Which one is higher than the other? Which one is the best?*

There are three orders, or three choirs of God's Angels and I will list them from high to low. The first Order includes:

- Seraphim
- Cherubim
- Thrones

For by Him all things were created, both in the heavens and on earth, visible and invisible, whether throners or dominions or rulers or authorities—all things have been created through Him and for Him. (Colossians 1:16)

The second Order consists of Dominions, Virtues, and Powers.

When He had disarmed the rulers and authorities, He made a public display of them, having triumphed over them through Him. (Colossians 2:15)

who is at the right hand of God, having gone into heaven, after angels and authorities and powers had been subjected to Him. (1 Peter 3:22)

There are powers in the air; there is a prince of the powers of the air, so we know they are organized. Their purpose is to block or disallow things that traverse through the atmosphere. Those things are blessings from God to man. They are answers to prayers from God to man.

So that the manifold wisdom of God might now be made known through the church to the rulers and the authorities in the heavenly places. (Ephesians 3:10)

in which you formerly walked according to the course of this world, according to the prince of the power of the air, of the spirit that is now working in the sons of disobedience. (Ephesians 2:2)

The third level or Order is Principalities, Archangels, Angels.

A little about each: the first sphere of Angels, the highest to lowest. The first choir or sphere of Angels supports the Godhead and the universe. The second sphere supports the cosmos. The third sphere supports the world we live in.

In the first choir or the first sphere are the Seraphim which are also called "burning ones." Their job is to worship God. Cherubim cover, protect and guard. God travels on Thrones. Yes, God's chariot is alive; it is made of Angels.

The second tier of Angels are Dominions who are over and regulating the duties of other Angels. Virtues bring forth miracles. And, **powers** live between the first and second heavens to stop evil demons in the world.

Saints of God, as we are set in Dominion what is our relationship to Angels? We don't worship angels, we don't serve them. Angels are in service to man and they obey the voice of the Word of God when spoken from Dominion and in Dominion. We are set on high to have Dominion.

Regarding fallen angels: God gave man the Earth. When someone is in your house or your realm, they are under your authority. Not that you have to take care of them, unless they are your minor children or others that the Lord has given you charge over. But those in your realm or under your authority must obey your authority. Be sure to walk in your authority and speak from that position. Man has authority over all the created works of God's hands and in Christ we can speak to entities that are in our realm, because we are to be the boss of this realm. God gave the Earth to man.

In the third choir there are Principalities, also known as Rulers; their job is to protect religions. Archangels are guardians overall, and of course, Angels are closest to man and sometimes can take on the appearance of a man. From the Bible we know that Archangels are such as Michael and Gabriel. They have an individual name therefore we may assume they are one. It is more likely that they are the leader or the captain over others. Powers and principalities are an aggregate of entities, not just one single *spirit.* The powers around a Throne make up the Throne for example. None of these are to be toyed with.

Some say don't do any warfare against a principality unless it is messing with you first. Others say don't do any warfare individually against a principality at all. And I've heard still another say, as long as you are covered with the Blood of Jesus, it is okay. For those who don't know, the backlash is supposed to be very devastating to deadly when you mess with spiritual things that you do not have authority to mess with.

Man is himself set in Dominion, crowned with Glory and honor. God bestows on him **Power** to get wealth, which is the lowest of all the powers. Love is the greatest power and money is the lowest. If we can't master the lowest power, then what can God trust us with?

THRONE, GATE, AND ALTAR -- THE HIERARCHY OF POWER

Scripture uses multiple structural images for authority. They are not interchangeable. A throne is not a gate. A gate is not an altar. Each represents a different level of jurisdiction. If we confuse them, we will misread spiritual power.

The Throne has Supreme Jurisdiction. A throne represents ultimate governing authority. The right to issue binding decree. Final judgment. The highest court of appeal. The source of law within a realm

A throne determines what is lawful. It does not request compliance. It commands it. Heaven has a throne. Nations have thrones. The heart has a throne. Thrones sit at the top of jurisdiction.

The Gate controls access and influence. In ancient cities, the gate was the place of counsel, judgment, negotiation, trade, and decision-making. Elders sat in the gate. Cases were heard in the gate. Transactions were ratified in the gate. A gate does not originate law; it administers it within a locality.

Spiritually speaking, a gate represents access points, places of influence, points of entry, places where authority is exercised but not originated.

This is why Scripture speaks of "the gates of hell. The Bible says the gates of hell shall not prevail. The psalmist commanded, "Lift up your heads, O gates." Gates determine who enters and what exits. Gates do not create the throne; they answer to it.

The altar is the place of covenant and exchange. An altar represents a place of sacrifice, covenant ratification, exchange, devotion, and worship. Altars do not rule; they establish agreement. What is offered at an altar determines allegiance. Altars can align with a rightful throne or with a counterfeit one. There are Godly altars. There are also evil altars. Any altar not sanctioned and sanctified by God is considered evil.

This is why idolatry always involves altars. And why covenant renewal involves altars. The altar is where allegiance is formalized. The throne is where allegiance is enforced.

Of thrones, gates and altars here is the hierarchy listed in order of authority, highest first.

1. **Throne** is the governing source.

2. **Gate allows a**dministrative access.

3. **Altar** is the place of covenant alignment.

An altar can align with a throne. A gate can enforce a throne's decree. But neither replaces the throne. If a counterfeit altar is built, it may shift allegiance.

If a gate is compromised, influence may enter, but the throne determines ultimate rule.

Many believers attempt to address throne-level problems at gate level. Or altar-level issues as though they were throne disputes. Confusion of hierarchy leads to misplaced warfare.

If the throne is secure, gates can be reclaimed. If allegiance is corrected at the altar, authority realigns. But if we mistake influence for sovereignty, we exaggerate darkness. The throne remains central; everything else is downstream.

Word curses for example are altar-level agreements. Territorial influences are gate-level dynamics. Heart allegiance can be affected by altar and throne interaction.

Throne, Gate, Altar — and Crown; clarifying the Hierarchy of Power.

- The **throne** is the seat of ultimate jurisdiction.
- The **gate** is the place of administrative access and influence.
- The **altar** is the site of covenant alignment and exchange.

Now we add another distinction so there is no confusion: The crown.

The crown is visible authority. A crown represents recognized authority. Honor. Public acknowledgment of rule. Reward or inheritance. Delegated governance.

A crown is worn.

A throne is occupied.

A crown signifies authority granted or acknowledged.

A throne signifies authority exercised.

A person may wear a crown and still not possess ultimate jurisdiction. A king may be crowned — but the throne determines the realm.

In Revelation, elders cast their crowns before the throne.

Why?

Because visible authority must answer to ultimate authority.

Crowns are derivative.

Thrones are governing.

The hierarchy in order. In descending order of authority:

1. **Throne** — Source of law and final decree

2. **Crown** — Recognized or delegated authority

3. **Gate** — Administrative enforcement and access

4. **Altar** — Covenant alignment and exchange

The altar establishes allegiance.

The gate administers influence.

The crown displays authority.

The throne determines law.

When these are confused, spiritual understanding becomes unstable.

No throne cannot be commanded by one who does not possess jurisdiction. Authority flows downward — not upward. No created being commands the Eternal Throne. No human legislates Heaven. Scripture never depicts believers ordering God, nor Jesus, nor the Holy Spirit. Angels are sent by God, not by men. We can ask; we don't demand or command. Even in bold prayer, we may appeal; but we do not legislate.

However, Scripture does show that Believers are invited to approach the Throne.

"Let us therefore come boldly to the throne of grace…" Hebrews

Boldness is not control; It is access. Approach is not command; it is petition. This distinction protects both reverence and confidence.

Attempting to command a throne is not wise. When someone attempts to: Demand from Heaven, issue decrees independent of alignment, treat Divine authority as mechanical power, or speak as though they originate jurisdiction, they repeat the pattern of usurpation. The first rebellion said, "I will ascend."

Unauthorized command is elevation language. The sons of Sceva in Acts attempt to exercise authority without alignment. The result is exposure.

Delegated authority functions only within relationship and obedience. It is not seized; it is entrusted.

Authority operates by alignment, not assertion. A Believer may bind and loose in alignment with heaven. Speak in the name of Christ under commission. Enforce what has already been decreed. But they do not create decree. Rewrite jurisdiction, or ever attempt to command the Eternal Throne.

Approach is granted.

Control is not.

Bold faith and presumptuous ambition are far from the same things. Never attempt to operate at throne level prematurely. Never confuse spiritual confidence with sovereignty. Never overestimate or overstep jurisdiction.

Never underestimate rightful access.

Thrones are not seized. They are either inherently possessed as with God, Delegated as with created ranks, Or aligned with as with redeemed believers. No one ascends by ambition.

Authority is received through obedience.

Abraham fighting the five kings is not just a rescue story. It is a throne conflict — and a jurisdictional test — long before Sinai, long before monarchy, long before Israel exists as a nation.

GOD IS ALREADY ENTHRONED

God does not become enthroned because humans enthrone Him. He is already enthroned. So, when the psalmists say things like:

- "Exalt the Lord our God"
- "Enthrone Him with praise"
- "Lift Him up"

They are not describing a change in God's status, they are describing a change in human recognition and alignment.

God's Throne is already established. The Psalms themselves affirm this repeatedly.

> The Lord has established His throne in heaven, and His kingdom rules over all. (Psalm 103:19)

God's Throne is not created by worship; it is recognized by worship.

Saying, "Enthrone Him" Means Public Acknowledgment. When worship language says "enthrone Him," it means declare Him king here. It is covenant language that says, we acknowledge your rule. We submit to your authority. We align our lives with your throne.

It is similar to a coronation ceremony. A king may already be the rightful heir, but the coronation publicly acknowledges the rule that was already true.

Praise establishes recognition of **His** rule.

Enthroned on the praises of Israel (Psalm 22:3).

This does not mean praise builds a literal throne for God, it means praise creates the environment where His rule is recognized and honored. In other words, praise does not establish God's Throne in Heaven .It establishes His rule in the worshiping community.

Worship reorders the human throne. When people exalt God, they are dethroning pride, dethroning idols, dethroning fear, and dethroning self. They are making room for the rightful king. So, the psalmists are not changing Heaven. They are changing the alignment of the earth and the heart.

5. Psalms Use Participatory Language

The Psalms invite people into participation.

That is why the language is full of commands like:

- "Magnify the Lord with me"
- "Lift up your heads, O gates"

- "Bless the Lord, O my soul"

These commands do not increase God's power, they increase awareness of His power.

The difference between ontology and acknowledgment. Theologically we can say, God is ontologically enthroned — by nature and by right. But He is relationally enthroned when people recognize and submit to His rule. The Psalms are about that second dimension.

The conflict of thrones is not about God competing for authority. It is about whether people acknowledge the authority that already exists. The psalmists are calling people to align their world with the throne that already stands in Heaven.

God is not enthroned by worship; He is already enthroned. Worship is the act by which human hearts and communities recognize the throne that has always stood. The real question is never whether God reigns. The real question is whether we recognize His reign.

A king in Israel usually had two recognitions of authority: Divine appointment (God's choice). Public acknowledgment (the people's acceptance). Both mattered, but they were not equal. God's choice established the right to rule, while the people's acceptance affected the stability of the rule.

Divine Anointing gives the right to rule. When someone was anointed by a prophet, it meant God had chosen them. For example, David is anointed by Samuel in 1 Samuel 16.

At that moment, David becomes the legitimate king in God's eyes. But he does not immediately rule Israel. In fact, he spends years fleeing Saul. So, the anointing established God's decision, not immediate political control.

Public recognition brings the stability of rule. Later, the tribes of Israel come to David and say, "We are your bone and flesh." Then they anoint him again as king in 2 Samuel 5. This second anointing isn't because God changed His mind.

It is the nation acknowledging what God had already established. So, David's kingship moved through stages:

1. Chosen by God
2. Anointed privately
3. Recognized gradually
4. Finally accepted by the nation

Acceptance by the people matters. Even when God appoints a ruler, human society still operates through loyalty, allegiance, obedience, and covenant.

If people refuse a king, the king may still be legitimate — but the kingdom becomes unstable. You see this repeatedly in Israel: Rehoboam loses ten tribes. Northern Israel repeatedly rejects kings. Civil wars erupt. So, legitimacy and acceptance are different things.

God establishes the true throne, but humans must decide whether they will align with it. A throne can exist without recognition, but rule becomes effective when allegiance aligns.

The pattern continues with Christ. The New Testament presents the same dynamic. Jesus is declared king by God:

All authority in heaven and on earth has been given to me.

Sometimes the world does not immediately recognize that rule. So, Christ's kingship is legitimate now, recognized partially, and will be fully acknowledged in the future: Every knee will bow. Philippians

That's universal recognition of a throne that already exists. God's anointing establishes the right to rule, but the people's allegiance determines the peace of the rule. When the psalmists say "exalt Him" or "enthrone Him," they are essentially saying, Recognize the king God has already established.

The throne is already there. The question is whether people will align with it.

DARK KINGDOM HIERARCHY

The following lists the main *spirits* of the dark kingdom. As a warning, do not rail against dignities. Any power or entity is in place because God allows it.

Unclean or *evil spirits* - Cause defilement. Defilement places a man outside the Gate. If you are not connected or cannot enter into the Courts of the Lord, or into worship, then how will you access Wisdom? How will you access Wealth?

There are heathen whose job is to heap up wealth, but we are talking about wealth from God, not counterfeit blessings--, those are traps. Like the old folks used to say, "Every dollar ain't a good dollar." So, don't accept money just because it is money. Are there strings attached? Where did this money come from? How much will it cost to pay it back? Can it be paid back? Like ever?

Principalities and **powers** - Higher ranking entities that influence regions or nations. As the enemy can block answers to prayers, he would use powers based on what is asked, how it impacts the

Kingdom of Heaven, the Earth, and based on who is praying to God.

Spirits of infirmity - Associated with afflictions and chronic ailments. Not only do people not feel like doing the usual things such as working or earning abundance when they are ill, sicknesses, diseases and disorders do the opposite of making wealth for people; they drain wealth through doctor's visits, co-pays, medicines, and lost time from work.

Seducing spirits - Promote lying doctrines to lead people into *error* and away from the Truth of God. Making bad decisions is a hallmark of the *spirit of error.*

Familiar spirits - Imitate deceased people and by other means provide occultic, second heaven knowledge. This can be a direct impact against your soul by way of your emotions.

Lying spirits - Incite or propagate deception, including false prophecy. Lying *spirits* put people in wrong places, wrong connections, and further into *error.* ***Spirit of antichrist*** - Opposes and denies the person and work of Christ. (Some say Ruling *spirits* are the 7th category.)

I will not speak much more with you, for the ruler of the world is coming, and he has nothing in Me;
(John 14:30)

Notice there are seven of these *spirits*. They travel in clusters. They travel in packs. A person is not likely to have just one; they are likely to have a group of them--, even groups of the seven types.

As I warn people not to play with God; don't get saved so you can *say* you're saved and then go out and sin like a fiend. God is not mocked. Don't go for deliverance and get partially delivered and not complete the process. Once delivered do not fail to maintain your deliverance; else your problems will get worse.

When the unclean spirit is gone out of a man, he walketh through dry places, seeking rest, and findeth none.

Then he saith, I will return into my house from whence I came out; and when he is come, he findeth it empty, swept, and garnished.

Then goeth he, and taketh with himself seven other spirits more wicked than himself, and they enter in and dwell there: and the last state of that man is worse than the first. Even so shall it be also unto this wicked generation. (Matthew 12:43-45)

The Scripture makes mention of all these types of entities but does not confine demons to just one "type." All of these types of devils, demons, *spirits*, fallen angels, idols and idol *gods* are destructive to man.

Regarding #2, a principality was sent to oppose Daniel to block his answer to prayers. The Archangel

Michael was sent to oppose that principality once Daniel had fasted and prayed for 21 days. That fact that it took 21 days of fasting and a whole Archangel to oppose a principality should inform you as to whether you want to accost a principality in warfare or not.

> But the prince of the kingdom of Persia was withstanding me for twenty-one days; then behold, Michael, one of the chief princes, came to help me, for I had been left there with the kings of Persia.
> (Daniel 10:13)

> Then he said, "Do you understand why I came to you? But I shall now return to fight against the prince of Persia; so I am going forth, and behold, the prince of Greece is about to come. (Daniel 10:20)

The Bible strongly suggests that the kingdom of darkness operates with structures of authority that mirror Heavenly order, but they are corrupted, temporary, and subordinate to God's sovereignty.

There are dark authorities that function like thrones — but Scripture rarely calls them that directly. The Bible Describes a Hierarchy of Dark Authority. The clearest text is Ephesians 6:12:

> For we wrestle not against flesh and blood, but against principalities, against powers, against the rulers of the darkness of this world, against spiritual wickedness in high places.

Four levels appear here: Principalities, Powers, Rulers of darkness, Spiritual wickedness in high places. This language implies layers of authority, not random demons. These are governmental terms, not creature descriptions.

Satan Possesses a "Throne." One place where Scripture *explicitly* uses the word throne in connection with darkness is Revelation 2:13. Speaking to the church in Pergamum:

> I know thy works, and where thou dwellest, even where Satan's throne is.

That implies a seat of authority, a center of influence, possibly a territorial stronghold. Scripture does not say Satan has a throne in heaven. His throne appears on earth, tied to a place of influence.

Satan Offers Jesus "The Kingdoms of the World. In the wilderness temptation (Matthew 4:8-9):

> "The devil taketh him up into an exceeding high mountain, and sheweth him all the kingdoms of the world…
> And saith unto him, All these things will I give thee…"

This reveals something about the dark kingdom. It claims governance over earthly systems. Not ownership — but influence. Jesus does not dispute that Satan exercises real authority in the present age. But it is borrowed time authority.

Daniel Reveals Territorial Spiritual Rulers. One of the most revealing passages is Daniel 10. An angel explains why he was delayed:

"The Prince of the kingdom of Persia withstood me twenty-one days…"

Later he mentions:

"the Prince of Greece shall come."

These "princes" are not human kings; they are spiritual authorities connected to earthly regions or systems. This strongly suggests organized dark governance.

Darkness mimics Heaven. The kingdom of darkness does not invent structure. It copies heaven. If heaven has Thrones, Authorities, Orders of angels, and Governance, then darkness attempts to mirror that system in corrupted form. But it is always counterfeit rule.

Scripture avoids calling them thrones. This is important theologically. The Bible is careful not to give darkness too much dignity. Heaven has Thrones, dominions, principalities, powers (Colossians 1:16). Darkness is described mostly with principalities, rulers, authorities-- but rarely thrones.

Why?

Because throne language belongs to true sovereignty. Darkness rules through deception, rebellion, illegitimate authority, and temporary dominion, not rightful kingship.

Christ has already disarmed them. The decisive statement comes in Colossians 2:15:

> Having disarmed principalities and powers, he made a public spectacle of them, triumphing over them in it.

This means that the hierarchy exists, but its legal authority was broken at the Cross. What remains is rebellion, not sovereignty. The kingdom of darkness organizes itself in structures that resemble thrones, but they are not true thrones. They are counterfeit seats of influence sustained by deception and rebellion.

Heaven has true thrones. Darkness has counterfeit rule. Heaven governs by authority. Darkness governs by usurpation. One is eternal order. The other is temporary rebellion.

IS A PRINCIPALITY DIFFERENT FROM A THRONE?

In Scripture (Ephesians 6), "principalities" refers to structured, high-level authorities — governing influences within the unseen realm. They are organized, hierarchical, derivative, operating within limits, never sovereign. A principality is not random evil. It is structured counterfeit governance.

Can a person "be involved in" a principality? No, not in the sense of *becoming* one. Humans are not principalities. But a person can align with one. A person could serve the interests of one, enforce the agenda of one. They could provide ground for a principality or become influenced by one. Remember hierarchy: throne to crown to gate, to altar. A principality is **throne-level** in its structure. The principality is counterfeit, but it ranks high.

A human being typically operates at gate or altar level. Gates and altars can serve thrones.

This can happen when a person becomes *entangled* with dark governance through persistent allegiance (ideological or spiritual). It could happen with covenant alignment, knowingly or unknowingly. It could happen by systemic injustice participation. Repeated agreement with lies or idolatrous loyalty. Authority abuse is usually not sudden; it is often gradual.

Dark structures operate through systems, narratives, culture, power consolidation, and or fear enforcement. When a person stabilizes and advances those structures, they are functioning as an *extension* — not as the principality itself.

Not every sin equals principality involvement, so don't overestimate what you are looking at or dealing with. Some power structures genuinely reflect organized evil, so don't underestimate what you may be looking at or dealing with. Scripture allows for both personal sin and structural evil.

For example, a ruler who oppresses for gain may be operating under a counterfeit throne structure. Or a culture that normalizes injustice may reflect principality-level influence. A spiritual leader who consistently manipulates through fear may be reinforcing a counterfeit hierarchy. Influence and alignment are not the same as transformation.

A human does not become a principality; but they can become aligned with one. That is a very dangerous person. Principalities require human cooperation. They do not function independently in earthly systems.

Authority transfers through agreement. Counterfeit thrones gain access through allegiance. Remove allegiance — and their reach contracts. A person does not *become* a principality. But a person can align with one — and enforce its agenda.

Principalities are structured, high-level spiritual authorities (created beings or offices). Humans are humans and remain humans. They are embodied image-bearers with delegated dominion on Earth.

These categories do not merge. There is no Biblical support for humans "becoming" principalities. But Scripture does show humans cooperating with, empowering, or enforcing dark structures. They are what I call in my books, teachings and prayers, **evil human agents**, those who are aligned with the kingdom of darkness and allowing or facilitating its agenda in the Earth against humans.

Alignment through authority delegation. In Genesis, humanity was given dominion over the Earth. That dominion was real. When allegiance shifted in Eden, jurisdiction was affected.

Paul later calls Satan, "the ruler of this world" "the god of this age" That language implies influence over systems — not ownership of Creation. How does that influence function? Through human alignment.

Principalities require cultural, political, religious, economic, and ideological systems and narratives. Humans stabilize those systems.

Without human cooperation, dark structures lose enforcement authority on Earth.

Biblical examples of human alignment. We see this pattern in Pharaoh hardening his heart (structural oppression). We see it in Babylon (imperial idolatry + political power). We see it in Herod seeking to destroy the Messiah. It is seen in religious leaders that resist Christ. These are not people "possessed by principalities, they are people enforcing dark governance through authority and decision.

Theologically, however, this is participation in principality-level influence.

Humans align with dark governance through ideological agreement, power preservation, fear of loss, material gain, pride, control. Principalities offer stability and reward for compliance.

This is why Scripture says, *The whole world lies under the power of the evil one.* Not because every individual is consciously devoted to evil — but because systems operate under counterfeit governance when allegiance is misplaced.

We must avoid demonizing every political disagreement, labeling individuals as agents of principalities, or treating structural evil as mystical obsession.

The New Testament never commands believers to identify specific territorial principalities by name. It commands faithfulness, resistance, obedience, truth, prayer, and righteous conduct.

Alignment with Christ displaces counterfeit alignment.

Principalities function at counterfeit throne-level structure. Humans function at gate and altar level. Through allegiance and decree, gates can serve thrones. Through covenant alignment, altars can reinforce thrones. But the Eternal Throne remains above all.

In summary, a human cannot become a principality. But a human can serve a principality's agenda. Enforce its structure. Stabilize its influence. Or resist and expose it. Authority flows through alignment. That's the consistent Biblical principle.

THRONES, DOMINIONS, PRINCIPALITIES

If God's Throne is uncreated, then every other throne is derivative. Scripture makes this distinction unmistakable.

In Colossians, speaking of Christ, it says:

> For by Him all things were created, in heaven and on earth, visible and invisible, whether thrones or dominions or principalities or powers — all things were created through Him and for Him.

The language is layered.

Thrones.
Dominions.
Principalities.
Powers.

These describe structured authority within Creation. Notice what the text establishes immediately: These thrones were created. That means that they are not eternal. They do not originate authority. They exist because Christ willed them into being. They exist for Him. This alone dismantles both angel worship and spiritual paranoia. No created throne rivals the Eternal Throne. It is sustained.

Scripture does not always separate rank from personality. Some authority structures appear to be Intelligent beings entrusted with jurisdiction. Offices are seats of governance that can be occupied.

In Daniel, we see "princes" associated with territories.

In Revelation, we see Angels associated with churches.

In Ephesians, we see principalities and powers referenced as structured authority.

These may function as both personal intelligences and assigned jurisdictions. Authority in heaven is not random; it is administered.

Delegated does not mean independent. The danger in reading about thrones, dominions, and principalities is overestimating their autonomy. Delegated authority operates only within assigned limits. A governor does not *own* the nation.

A judge does not write the constitution. An ambassador does not establish foreign policy. All operate within higher rule. Likewise, every created throne answers upward.

None generate their own legitimacy. This prevents two errors: Fear of spiritual hierarchies, and fascination with them. They are structured, yes-- but they are subordinate.

Authority reflects the one who assigns it. Because Christ created "thrones or dominions or principalities or powers," their existence reflects His order. Hierarchy is not evil. Structure is not oppressive. Rank is not corruption. Corruption occurs when delegated authority forgets its source. Rebellion does not invent hierarchy; it distorts it.

Created authority is originally good. Otherwise, when we later examine counterfeit thrones, we risk assuming that all structure is suspect, or that all authority is oppressive or corrupt. Scripture does not teach thus. It teaches that authority is good when aligned. Authority becomes destructive when severed from Godly origin.

Not all thrones are evil. Some are faithful. Some are obedient. Some operate in perfect submission to the Eternal Throne.

Christ ranks above all attempts at usurpation.

He is before all things, and in Him all things hold together. (Colossians 1:17)

The ranks exist within Him. They are sustained by Him. They are accountable to Him. Which means when rebellion enters the story, it is not a clash between equal powers; it is a fracture within created order. The Eternal Throne remains untouched.

THE FIRST USURPATION

It is an abomination to kings to commit wickedness: for the throne is established by righteousness. (Proverbs 16:12)

Authority existed before rebellion. Structure existed before distortion. Which means rebellion did not introduce power into the universe; it challenged it.

Scripture does not give us a documentary account of pre-human rebellion, but it does give us prophetic language that reveals the pattern of usurpation.

In Isaiah 14, addressing the king of Babylon, the prophet records words that exceed earthly ambition:

You said in your heart, 'I will ascend to heaven; I will raise my throne above the stars of God… I will make myself like the Most High. (Isaiah 14:13)

I will raise my throne.

Rebellion is not dissatisfaction; it is self-elevation. It is the attempt to occupy a seat not assigned. It is ambition against origin.

Similarly, in Ezekiel 28, addressing the king of Tyre, the prophet speaks in imagery that again stretches beyond ordinary human pride:

> "You were in Eden, the garden of God… You were an anointed guardian cherub… Your heart was proud because of your beauty." (Ezekiel 28:13)

Whether these passages refer directly to a pre-Adamic rebellion or employ typology through earthly rulers, the pattern is unmistakable: Privilege precedes pride. Delegated authority forgets its source. Beauty becomes self-reference. Assignment becomes aspiration. Rebellion begins internally.

"You said in your heart."

Before there was an outward conflict, there was inward elevation. The first usurpation was conceived in thought.

Usurpation requires imagination. Authority cannot be seized without first being imagined as attainable. The rebel does not deny the throne exists. He seeks to ascend to it.

Rebellion is rivalry. It acknowledges the throne — and attempts to rival it. This is why rebellion is always personal. It is not merely structural disagreement. It is a contest of supremacy.

The pattern repeats in Eden. When we arrive in Genesis 3, the pattern is already familiar. The serpent does not introduce new authority. He questions existing authority.

"Did God really say…?"

That question is not informational. It is jurisdictional. It implies that God's decree may be negotiable, or that the boundary may be flexible. It then concludes that the Throne may be contested.

Then comes the promise: "You will be like God." Elevation again. Not survival. Not curiosity. Ascension. Human rebellion mirrors the earlier pattern. Authority is not denied; it is challenged.

Usurpation is always suggestion first. Notice how rebellion operates; it does not begin with force. It begins with speech. It does not overthrow immediately. It persuades.

The throne is not seized by violence first. It is surrendered by agreement. In Heaven, a heart said, "I will ascend." In Eden, a voice said, "You will be like." In both cases, rebellion required internal consent. Authority transfers through alignment.

The usurpation failed. No created being can originate authority. The Throne being challenged was uncreated. Which means rebellion was structurally doomed. Delegated authority cannot become original authority. It can only detach from it. Once detached, it loses its sustaining source. This is why Scripture never presents rebellion as an equal war. It presents it as defiance within a created order. The Eternal Throne remains untouched.

The first conflict was not about territory. It was about position; it was about supremacy. Rebellion does not begin with armies; it begins with *"I will."* That phrase echoes through history.

Every later throne conflict follows the same pattern: Internal elevation. Suggestion against decree. Promise of autonomous ascent. Misplaced allegiance. We will see this pattern again in the wilderness. We will see it another time at the Cross, and again wherever human hearts enthrone themselves.

We won't misunderstand the first usurpation, or we will misunderstand every later one. Rebellion is not innovation; it is imitation. It does not create a throne; it attempts to replicate one. And it can only function where authority is forgotten or denied.

The Eternal Throne was not shaken. But lesser thrones were corrupted, and the conflict of thrones entered history.

THRONES OF DARKNESS

If God's Throne is uncreated and created thrones are delegated, then counterfeit thrones must be understood as distortions of structure — not rivals of origin. Scripture does not present darkness as chaotic anarchy. It presents it as organized rebellion.

For we do not wrestle against flesh and blood, but against principalities, against powers, against the rulers of the darkness of this world, against spiritual wickedness in high places. (Ephesians 6:10-12)

The language is governmental: principalities, powers, rulers, and darkness imitate structure. It does not invent hierarchy; it corrupts it.

Counterfeit does not mean equal. This must be settled immediately. A counterfeit throne is not an equal throne. It remains unauthorized. It is derivative, sustained only within limits, and operating on borrowed time. Dark authority does not create law. It exploits it. It does not originate jurisdiction. It occupies abandoned ground.

The moment Christ is revealed in Revelation, the false structure trembles. This is because it was always temporary and in no way equal.

When Daniel speaks of a "prince of Persia" resisting for twenty-one days, he reveals something significant. Darkness can operate in layers. There are ranks. There are territorial influences. There are structured resistances.

But even there, the narrative makes something clear: Assistance comes from higher authority. The delay is not defeat. The outcome is never uncertain. Organization does not equal sovereignty.

Dark thrones function by mimicking Divine order. They demand allegiance. They promise protection. They enforce fear. They punish dissent. They reward compliance.

Every counterfeit throne attempts to present itself as necessary. It survives by persuasion more than force. This is consistent with the first usurpation. Rebellion does not overthrow the Eternal Throne. It persuades lesser authorities to detach from it.

It's occupation is temporary. In the wilderness, the tempter tells Jesus,

All this authority I will give You… for it has been delivered to me.

Delivered. That word is telling. It implies transfer — not origin. Dark authority operates where something was yielded. It rules where something was surrendered. It governs where agreement has been granted. But it does not own, and it does not create.

Darkness feels strong. Counterfeit thrones feel powerful because they operate within structured systems. They influence cultures. They shape institutions. They exploit fear. They capitalize on human allegiance. But power felt is not power ultimate.

Scripture never depicts darkness as structurally equal to Heaven. It depicts it as parasitic. It must attach. It must influence. It must persuade. It cannot self-sustain.

> Having disarmed principalities and powers, He made a public spectacle of them, triumphing over them in it. (Colossians 2:15)

Notice the language. Disarmed. Not annihilated in that moment — but stripped. The exposure matters. Dark authority depends on concealment. When revealed, its legitimacy collapses. The Cross was not merely for our personal forgiveness; it was structural exposure.

Every counterfeit throne is subject to the Eternal One. Darkness does not own history; it disrupts it. Every disruption eventually answers upward.

HOW COUNTERFEIT THRONES GAIN ACCESS

Counterfeit thrones do not create territory, but they do gain access to it. Dark authority does not originate jurisdiction. It exploits openings within created order. Scripture consistently presents rebellion as functioning through agreement, never through ultimate sovereignty.

Authority flows through alignment. Access is gained through allegiance. When Adam was given dominion in Genesis, it was real. Delegated. Meaningful.

When he disobeyed, the issue was not merely moral failure. It was jurisdictional transfer.

Paul later calls Satan "the *god* of this age." Not because he created the age. But because allegiance shifted. Access was granted. Darkness does not take dominion where no authority was given. It operates where allegiance is misplaced.

Access can be granted through decree. Words matter in Scripture because they formalize alignment.

When a king issued a decree in the ancient world, it established law. Similarly, when authority is verbally affirmed, covenantally enacted, or persistently agreed with, it stabilizes influence.

This is why Scripture warns repeatedly about vows, oaths, covenants, agreements, and spoken declarations. Words are legal; they ratify allegiance.

Access can be gained through idolatry is throne displacement. When something created is elevated above the Creator, jurisdiction shifts. Paul writes in Romans that humanity "exchanged the glory of the immortal God" for created images.

Exchange is economic language. Something is surrendered. Something is enthroned. Idolatry is a transaction of authority.

Fear is misplaced trust, and access can be gained through that fear.

What I greatly feared has come upon me. (Job 3:25)

Fear aligns expectation with darkness rather than promise with God. Where fear governs, authority is misdirected. Darkness enforces through intimidation because intimidation destabilizes allegiance. If confidence in rightful rule collapses, counterfeit rule feels necessary.

Access can be attained through injustice and bloodshed. Scripture presents another sober pattern: Blood speaks. When Cain kills Abel, the Lord says:

> The voice of your brother's blood cries out to Me from the ground.

Violence (sin) creates testimony. Testimony creates grounds for judgment. Grounds create jurisdiction. This is not superstition. It is moral order. When injustice saturates a land, authority structures shift. Darkness exploits unrepented, unresolved sin and transgression. It must be repeated.

Access does not equal ultimate possession or ownership. Counterfeit thrones occupy; they do not create. They distort what already exists. Because they are derivative, their authority is always limited by higher decree. This is why repentance, covenant restoration, and obedience consistently dismantle dark influence.

Alignment reestablishes jurisdiction.

The pattern holds throughout Scripture: authority is assigned. If allegiance shifts, then counterfeit rule gains influence. Judgment exposes the illegitimate occupation. Restoration reorders the throne. This is governmental reality. Dark thrones gain access through agreement. They lose access through realignment.

The first usurpation organized counterfeit structures.

The Mechanics of Access

Counterfeit thrones can operate only until confronted by rightful authority. Nowhere is that confrontation clearer than in the Wilderness.

WHAT'S THE PROBLEM -- THRONE, GATE OR ALTAR?

How do you know if you have a throne level problem, a gate level problem or an altar level problem?

Throne, gate, and altar operate at three different layers of authority and access. When people confuse them, they often fight the wrong battle.

- **Altars** govern covenants and worship.
- **Gates** govern access and entry.
- **Thrones** govern authority and rulership.

Each produces a different type of problem.

ALTAR-LEVEL PROBLEMS - *(covenant, sacrifice, worship, allegiance)*

An altar is where something is offered and a covenant relationship is established or maintained. Biblically:

- Noah built an altar after the flood.

- Abraham built altars where God appeared to him.
- Elijah confronted the prophets of Baal at the altar on Mount Carmel.

Altars answer the question, “Who is being honored here?” Signs of an altar problem include repeated spiritual cycles that feel covenantal. When you see inherited patterns in a family line, these are altar level issues. Deep emotional or spiritual attachments that feel binding, or strange loyalty to something harmful, this is altar level. Patterns that seem tied to worship, devotion, or allegiance? Suspect **altar level** problems.

Examples are generational bondage, repeated relationship patterns, family spiritual agreements made long ago, or ancestral vows or dedications. These are usually altar issues because something was given or dedicated. Resolution normally involves repentance, renunciation, breaking agreements, and re-establishing rightful worship.

GATE-LEVEL PROBLEMS - *(access, permission, entry points)*

A gate is about who or what is allowed in. In Scripture, gates were the place of access and transaction. Cities had gates, elders judged at the gates, and enemies tried to capture gates first. Gates answer the question, “How did this get access?”

Signs of a gate problem are: sudden intrusions into a life, influence entering through relationships, spiritual oppression connected to a place or object, problems tied to access points. Such thigs are seen as unhealthy relationships opening influence, exposure through media or environments, spiritual harassment that began after contact with something.

Problems tied to a house, office, or location?

Gate issues are about entry permissions. Resolution often involves closing access points, removing objects or influences, ending relationships or environments that opened the door, prayerfully shutting the gate.

THRONE-LEVEL PROBLEMS - *(authority, rulership, jurisdiction).*

A throne is not about access or covenant — it is about who has the right to rule. A throne answers the question, "Who is governing here?"

Biblically, Solomon sat on the throne of Israel. Satan offered Jesus the kingdoms of the world (authority structures). God is described as seated on a Throne in Heaven. Thrones are governmental positions.

Signs of a throne problem: conflict over authority, someone trying to control, dominate, or rule, disputes about leadership or jurisdiction, systems or environments ruled by corruption. Examples:

- workplace power struggles
- institutional corruption
- leadership battles
- someone trying to take authority over your life.

Throne issues are about who sits in the seat.

Resolution usually involves rightful authority being restored, removing illegitimate rulership, stepping into rightful governance.

The easiest diagnostic question -- you can often tell the level by asking one question:

What is actually being contested?

If the issue is about: worship, allegiance, or covenant, then it's probably an altar issue. If it is about access, entry, or influence, then it's probably about a gate. If it is about authority, rule, governance, then it's most likely about a throne.

They can stack on top of each other. Many times, problems appear in layers. It could be an altar, gate, and or throne problem.

For example, an altar covenant creates spiritual permission. That permission opens a gate of access. Over time something establishes authority (a throne).

Sometimes the visible issue is a throne conflict, but the root is an altar problem.

Imagine a corrupt leader ruling a city. The possible layers are first a throne layer: the corrupt ruler governing the system. Then there could be a gate layer which is how the corruption enters the system. Add to that an altar layer, what the culture actually worships (money, power, etc.). The altar usually feeds the throne.

Altars attract thrones. Where worship is established, authority eventually forms. That is why in the Bible, Baal had altars and prophets. Kingdoms had thrones and cities had gates. They are different pieces of the same spiritual architecture.

The hierarchy of spiritual structures from lowest to highest:

1. altar
2. gate
3. throne
4. dominion / kingdom

This is serious: A problem moves up that ladder if it isn't dealt with early.

Men built altars in the Bible all the time, God told them to build an altar, more than once. Men were promoted to thrones, but whoever built a gate? Who was ever told to build a gate?

Men were told to build altars. Men were placed on thrones. But people were almost never told to build gates in the same spiritual sense. That's because gates are primarily structural, not devotional. They belong to cities and houses, not to worship.

Gates in Scripture were usually part of city walls, temple complexes, and houses or courtyards.

Bible examples:

- Nehemiah supervised the rebuilding of Jerusalem's walls and its gates after the exile.
- Solomon built temple courts and gates as part of the temple structure.

The command was not "build a gate;" the command was "build the city. Gates come automatically with a city. Gates are usually described, repaired, guarded, or judged at, rather than spiritually constructed.

In the Bible, gates are places of entry, transaction, judgment, and authority recognized by a community. In the Bible we'd see elders sat at the gate. Legal cases were heard there. Gates represent access points where authority is exercised. This is why Jesus said, "The gates of hell shall not prevail…"

Gates represent defensive strongholds of a system, not offensive attack points. And, of course, we've been discussing thrones throughout the book so you know what they do and how they function.

Now the weighty question is: How you pray or conduct yourself if an altar situation, a gate problem, or a throne issue is up against you? Each one requires a different posture.

Many Believers confuse them and fight the wrong way; we won't.

ALTAR SITUATION - *(covenant and worship problems)*

When the issue is altar-level, the question is: "What covenant or allegiance is operating here?" In Scripture the response was almost always repentance, renunciation, and restoring right worship.

For example, Elijah first repaired the altar of the Lord before confronting the prophets of Baal. He did not start with warfare. He restored the altar first.

The prayer posture is first, repentance, consecration, re-dedication, declaring rightful worship. Example prayer posture:

"Lord, any covenant or allegiance that is not aligned with You is renounced. I establish Your authority and worship in this place, in the Name of Jesus."

Altar problems are solved by alignment, not primarily confrontation.

<u>GATE SITUATION</u> - *(access and permission problems)*

Gate problems ask, "How did this gain entry?" In Scripture the response was usually closing, guarding, and removing access. For example, Nehemiah ordered the gates closed on the Sabbath so merchants could not enter. He did not debate them. He shut the gate.

The prayer posture is revoke permission, close access, and guard boundaries. Example posture:

"Every access point that allowed this influence is closed, in the Name of Jesus."

Often this involves practical action, not just prayer. Ending relationships. Leaving environments. Removing objects or influences.

<u>THRONE SITUATION</u> - *(authority and rulership problems)*

Throne issues ask, "Who has the right to govern here?" These are authority conflicts. Biblically, throne conflicts are resolved by judgment, removal of illegitimate authority, establishment of rightful authority. Example: God removes kings and raises others.

The prayer posture is to appeal to God's authority, declaration of rightful order, refusal to submit to illegitimate rule. Example posture:

"Lord, You establish and remove authority. Let rightful governance be established, in the Name of Jesus."

Throne problems are not solved by closing doors or repenting alone. They are resolved by governmental authority shifting.

Problems move up the ladder; they escalate when they are not dealt with early. The movement usually looks like this:

Stage 1 — Altar. A wrong covenant, worship, or allegiance begins. Example: A culture begins to worship money, power, or pleasure. At this stage it is still mostly devotional or cultural.

Stage 2 — Gate. Once allegiance is established, access opens. The culture now welcomes influences that serve that altar. Example: Media, policies, relationships, systems begin reinforcing it. Now the gate is open.

Stage 3 — Throne. Eventually the influence becomes institutional authority. Now laws, systems, and leaders reflect that allegiance. The altar has produced a throne.

Example pattern in Scripture. Israel repeatedly followed this sequence:

1. Altars to other *gods*
2. Foreign influence entering the land
3. Oppressive rulers or invading kingdoms

Pay very close attention here:

- **The altar created the gate.**
- **The gate allowed the throne.**
- **If someone fights only the throne but ignores the altar, the cycle returns.**

This is why prophets in Scripture often began with repentance, and tearing down altars. Thrones follow altars.

In many Biblical cities, altars, gates, and thrones were physically connected. Jerusalem had the temple altar, the city gates, and the royal throne.

This reflected the deeper order: worship to access, to governance

There is actually a fourth structure above thrones that scripture repeatedly refers to dominion / kingdoms. That is too deep to go into in this volume, but it explains why sometimes a throne can change but the system remains the same. That book is entitled, **Set On High to Have Dominion.**

THE WILDERNESS: INITIATION REFUSED

Every counterfeit throne seeks validation. It cannot originate authority, but it can attempt to recruit it. The wilderness temptation is not merely a test of appetite. It is a confrontation of thrones.

After His baptism, Jesus is led by the Spirit into the wilderness. He has just heard the declaration:

This is My beloved Son, in whom I am well pleased.

Identity has been publicly affirmed. Authority has been announced. Now comes the challenge.

If you are the Son of God…

The tempter begins not with bread, but with identity: "If You are the Son of God…" The phrase is not uncertainty. It is provocation. Sonship implies authority. Authority implies jurisdiction.

The question beneath the words is: Under whose authority will You operate?

Turn this stone into bread.

Command this stone to become bread.

The suggestion appears harmless. Bread is not immoral. Hunger is not sinful. Power is not illegitimate. But timing and source matter.

If Jesus had acted at that moment, under that suggestion, He would have exercised power without the Father's commission, in response to a rival voice, to satisfy immediate need, under pressure rather than obedience.

Power used outside authorization becomes misaligned, even if the outcome appears good. Authority is not measured by ability. It is measured by alignment.

Every kingdom is initiated through obedience. If Jesus had acted at the suggestion of the tempter, the act itself would have signaled alignment. The miracle would not have proven sonship. It would have demonstrated susceptibility.

The question was not: *Can You do this?* That initiation language. No, it was under whose authority *Will you do this?*

Counterfeit thrones seek participation. They seek cooperation. They seek consent. Jesus refuses.

Man shall not live by bread alone, but by every word that proceeds from the mouth of God.

This is not about carbohydrates. It is about source. Provision does not outrank obedience.

Stones are weapons, not food. Throughout Scripture, stones mark: judgment, covenant testimony, warfare, finality. Stones execute justice. Stones seal tombs. Stones mark boundaries.

They are instruments of decree, not sustenance. To turn stone into bread would have inverted categories. Weapons are not nourishment.

Judgment is not appetite. Authority is not consumption.

Jesus refuses to internalize what was meant to be wielded. He will not redefine instruments of warfare as personal provision.

The offer of Kingdoms was seen in the second temptation makes the confrontation explicit.

All this authority I will give You… for it has been delivered to me.

Delivered. Again, derivative language. The tempter offers accelerated enthronement. No cross. No suffering. No obedience unto death. Just recognition. But the cost is worship.

If You will bow down before me…

That is throne language. It is submission language; it is allegiance language.

Jesus answers:

You shall worship the Lord your God, and Him only shall you serve. (Luke 4:8)

Service reveals sovereignty. Worship reveals throne. There is no negotiation.

The pinnacle and public spectacle. The third temptation shifts to public display.

Throw Yourself down…

Spectacle is offered as proof. But authority does not prove itself through theatrics. It proves itself through obedience.

Jesus refuses to force Divine intervention for validation. He will not test the Father to prove sonship. He will not manipulate Heaven for display.

Angels came only after Jesus' obedience. Only after the confrontation concludes do the Gospels record:

Then the devil left Him, and behold, angels came and ministered to Him.

The Angels did not come before, or during; they came after. Assistance follows alignment. Jesus does not summon Angels. He remains submitted. Authority preserved through obedience invites rightful support.

The wilderness was not about resisting hunger. It was about refusing premature enthronement. It was about declining illegitimate initiation. It was about preserving alignment with the Eternal Throne.

Had Jesus acted under suggestion rather than commission, the miracle would have worked — but the authority would have shifted.

He refused.

The conflict of thrones in Jesus' Wilderness temptations was decided in Jesus' obedience.

Counterfeit thrones rarely announce themselves as evil. They offer acceleration, validation, relief, spectacle, and influence. But every offer carries the same question: Under whose authority will you act?

The wilderness reveals something foundational. Rightful authority is preserved not by power, but by **obedience**. Initiation into darkness requires only one thing: Agreement.

Jesus gave none.

THE CROSS: PUBLIC EXPOSURE OF THRONES

The wilderness preserved alignment.

The Cross exposed illegitimacy.

If the first usurpation began with internal elevation, and the wilderness confronted suggestion, the cross confronts structure. This is not merely execution; it is revelation.

Before the crucifixion, **Jesus** declares:

"Now is the judgment of this world; now will the ruler of this world be cast out." (John 12:31)

The language is decisive. Judgment. Ruler. Cast out. The Cross is not described as tragedy. It is described as tribunal. The throne conflict that began with "I will ascend" reaches public reckoning.

From the sixth hour to the ninth hour, darkness covers the land. This is not atmospheric detail. It is symbolic confrontation. Darkness attempts to eclipse Light. Note the boundary: The darkness does not remain. It does not redefine time. It does not blur covenant boundaries. It recedes. Creation responds — but it does not reverse. Darkness misreads silence as victory.

It does not understand obedience.

"It Is Finished"

When Jesus cries,

"It is finished,"

He is not expressing exhaustion. He is declaring completion. The Greek term carries the sense of fulfillment, accomplishment, payment rendered. Redemption is concluded before the Sabbath begins. Nothing spills over. Nothing remains pending.

The work ends in daylight. Authority does not rush against the clock. It concludes deliberately.

The veil is torn. At that moment the Earth quakes. Rocks split. The veil of the temple is torn from top to bottom. It is not torn by human initiative, but by Divine action. The tearing of the veil is Throne language. Access changes. Jurisdiction shifts.

The structure that once mediated Presence is reconfigured. This is constitutional reform, disarmed and displayed.

Having disarmed principalities and powers, He made a public spectacle of them, triumphing over them in it. (Colossians)

Disarmed, the weapon is removed. The legitimacy is exposed. Dark authority depends on concealment.

The Cross makes it visible. This is a spectacle. The humiliation of Christ becomes the humiliation of counterfeit rule. The throne that appeared dominant is shown to be derivative. Jesus, who the enemy thought he had made a spectacle of, becomes the spectacle.

The stone and the silence. He is laid in a tomb. A stone is rolled into place. The Sabbath begins. No miracles are performed. No public signs occur. Creation rests. The work is complete.

Healing ministries earlier in His life addressed individual bodies. The Cross addresses structural curse. Rest follows completion. Authority does not require constant demonstration.

Resurrection of Christ was His Heavenly enthronement. On the first day of the week, the stone is rolled away. Not to release Jesus or prove His defeat. But to reveal vacancy. Death has lost jurisdiction. The resurrection is not merely revival. Again, it makes spectacle of the plan of the enemy against Our Lord and Savior.

This, again, is enthronement language.

Later, He declares:

"All authority in heaven and on earth has been given to Me."

Given. Publicly affirmed. The throne conflict resolves not in negotiation, but in declaration. The Cross disarmed. The Resurrection enthroned.

The Cross is central to Throne-to-throne conflict. If the first rebellion said, "I will ascend," the Cross demonstrates that the way to rule is first descent. Obedience unto death exposes illegitimate elevation.

The throne of darkness collapses under sacrificial submission.

Authority that grasps fractures.

Authority that obeys endures.

At the Cross, counterfeit thrones were exposed. Illegitimate authority was stripped. Access was reconfigured. The Eternal Throne was vindicated publicly. The conflict of thrones did not begin there, but it was revealed there. The Cross did not create authority, but it displayed rightful authority.

Every throne since must answer to it.

And I will overthrow the throne of kingdoms, and I will destroy the strength of the kingdoms of the heathen; and I will overthrow the chariots, and those that ride in them; and the horses and their riders shall come down, every one by the sword of his brother. (Haggai 2:22)

AUTHORITY ENFORCED: AFTER THE CROSS

The Cross exposed counterfeit thrones. The resurrection declared rightful rule. But exposure alone does not reorder history. Authority must be exercised.

After rising, Jesus speaks with unmistakable clarity: **"All authority in heaven and on earth has been given to Me."**

All authority; not some or partial.

The statement is comprehensive. Heaven <u>and</u> Earth. The throne conflict is not suspended. It is resolved in declaration.

We see delegated enforcement here. Immediately after declaring His authority, He says: "Go therefore…" The "therefore" matters. Because He has all authority, they are *sent*. The Church does not create authority. It enforces delegated authority. There is no independent mandate. Only extension.

Believers do not operate as rival thrones. They operate under commission.

In Acts, we see this pattern repeatedly. A lame man is healed not by incantation, but by alignment:

"In the name of Jesus Christ of Nazareth, rise up and walk."

The "name" is not a magical phrase. It is legal representation. It signals delegated authority. The apostles do not say, "By our power." They say, "In His name."

Authority flows downward. It is not self-generated. Resistance continues. Enforcement does not eliminate resistance. Principalities still oppose. Systems still distort. Dark structures still attempt influence. But the posture changes.

Before the Cross, darkness confronted from a position of apparent leverage. After the Resurrection, it resists from a position of exposure. The difference is subtle but decisive. Resistance remains. Legitimacy does not.

There **is** danger in independent enforcement. Here is where many misunderstand. Delegated authority is powerful, but it is also bounded. When Believers attempt to operate outside alignment, outside obedience, or outside commission, they repeat the Wilderness mistake.

Power without authorization fractures. The sons of Sceva in Acts attempt to invoke the name without relationship. The result is humiliation.

Authority is not a tool. It is a trust.

Binding and Loosing is an authority we have been entrusted with. Jesus tells His Disciples:

“Whatever you bind on earth shall be bound in heaven, and whatever you loose on earth shall be loosed in heaven.”

This is enforcement language. Note the direction: Heaven establishes. Earth aligns. The Church does not invent decree; it ratifies what is already established. Binding and loosing are judicial terms. They reflect alignment with the throne — not independent legislation.

After ascending, Christ the King is described as seated at the Right Hand of the Father. Seated again. Rule is not frantic. It is established. Intercession is not insecurity. It is governance. The Church acts on Earth under a seated King, not under a struggling one.

Authority and enforcement after the Cross looks like: Obedience before action. Alignment before declaration. It is representation, not replacement. It is confidence without arrogance. It is resistance without fear. Counterfeit thrones still attempt influence. But they no longer operate undisclosed.

The Cross removed concealment.

The resurrection affirmed supremacy. Enforcement now flows from clarity. Authority is not theoretical; it is lived. Every act of obedience enforces rightful rule. Every refusal of counterfeit suggestion preserves alignment. Every proclamation made under Christ's name extends His Throne.

The conflict of Throne to thrones did not end at the Cross. It was settled there. And it is enforced wherever allegiance aligns with the risen King.

THE THRONE OF THE HEART

Heaven has a Throne. Nations have thrones. Darkness attempts to erect thrones. But the most contested throne in Scripture is not cosmic; it is internal. It is the heart.

Scripture does not treat the heart as the seat of emotion. It treats it as the seat of allegiance.

As a man thinks in his heart, so is he. (Proverbs)

Jesus teaches:

Out of the abundance of the heart the mouth speaks.

The heart is a governing center; it's not just for feelings; it is the inner seat of authority.

When the Bible commands:

Love the Lord your God with all your heart,

it is not asking for affection alone. It is demanding singular allegiance. The throne of the heart is the place from which: decisions are made, loyalties are established, trust is assigned, fear is permitted, and obedience is chosen. Every external conflict of thrones eventually becomes internal.

Who sits there? Someone must. Someone will. The heart cannot be vacant. A throne is never empty. If God is not enthroned in the heart, something else is. Things such as Self, Fear, ambition, wounds. It could be approval, security, or control. The absence of visible idolatry does not mean the absence of rule.

Something always governs.

Just as cosmic rebellion began with internal elevation — "I will ascend" — the heart mirrors that pattern. The inner usurper does not begin by rejecting God outright.

It begins by negotiating obedience. By redefining boundaries. By elevating preference over decree. The throne shifts quietly. Not through violence, but through agreement.

This is where earlier patterns converge. Words spoken over a person carry weight because the heart can ratify them. If a word is received as decree, it stabilizes influence. If a lie is enthroned, it governs behavior. If fear is given authority, it directs decision. The throne of the heart determines allegiance. It determines which voice is law.

Throughout Scripture, God promises something radical, circumcision of the heart.

I will give you a new heart.

This is not simply emotional healing language. It is governmental replacement. Covenant is not behavior modification; it is throne transfer. Salvation is not mere pardon. It is relocation of authority. The old seat is vacated. The rightful King is invited.

Jesus does not co-rule. The Cross disarmed counterfeit structures. But it is still up to the individual; the heart must still surrender. Jesus does not negotiate co-regency. He does not share the Throne with fear. He does not sit beside ambition. He reigns — or He is resisted. This is why discipleship feels costly. It is not about preferences. It is about position.

After the Cross, believers enforce authority externally. But first, they must enforce it internally. The wilderness temptation repeats in miniature in every life. We are presented with choices all the time. Do we act under suggestion? Do we act under temptation? Or do we act under commission?

Every decision reaffirms who sits on the throne of the heart.

The great cosmic conflict narrows to a singular question: Who rules you? The throne of the heart is the final jurisdiction. Every counterfeit throne seeks entry there. Every rightful decree seeks residence there. History bends toward the visible revelation of the

King. But allegiance is determined in the unseen seat within.

There was a Throne before Creation. There were delegated thrones. There was rebellion. There were counterfeit structures. There was confrontation. There was exposure. There was resurrection and then enthronement.

Now the choice is even more obvious.

The conflict of thrones continues. Man has free will, and allegiance is voluntary.

The Eternal Throne remains unshaken.

The question is whether the inner throne will align with it.

ABRAHAM AND THE FIVE KINGS: AUTHORITY WITHOUT AMBITION

Before Israel had a king, before there was a throne in Jerusalem, before there was a temple or monarchy, there was a man called by God.

In Genesis 14, Abraham hears that his nephew Lot has been taken captive in a regional war involving multiple kings. Five kings rise against four. Confederations form. Territory shifts. Power consolidates. This is political warfare**. It is throne conflict**. Abraham steps into it — without being a king.

Abraham fights without a crown. Abraham is not crowned. He does not rule a city. He is not enthroned, yet he gathers 318 trained men and defeats a coalition of kings.

This is extraordinary. A covenant man overcomes crowned rulers? Yes. How? Why? Because authority does not originate in crowns; it originates in alignment. Abraham's authority flows from promise, not position. He acts without throne ambition.

After the victory, the king of Sodom offers Abraham wealth saying, “Give me the persons, and take the goods for yourself.” Abraham refuses that king.

This is not generosity. It is an invitation to entanglement. If Abraham accepts, Sodom can claim: *“I made Abram rich.”*

That is throne language. It attempts to stabilize allegiance. Abraham refuses:

> I have lifted my hand to the Lord, God Most High…
> that I would not take a thread or a sandal strap…
> lest you should say, ‘I have made Abram rich.’

Abram will not allow a lesser throne to claim to be the source of his wealth. Abram fights and rescues Lot, but he does not transfer his allegiance.

Before the offer from Sodom, another figure appears: Melchizedek, King of Salem and priest of God Most High. He blesses Abraham. He brings bread and wine. He names the source of victory:

> Blessed be Abram by God Most High… who has
> delivered your enemies into your hand.

Abraham responds by giving him a tenth of all. This exchange is crucial. Abraham recognizes a higher order of authority. He gives tithe not to Sodom’s throne — but to the priestly king aligned with the Eternal Throne.

War precedes worship.

Victory precedes alignment reaffirmed.

The altar precedes consolidation of power.

Authority without usurpation: Abraham defeats kings but does not become one. He exercises authority but does not enthrone himself. He refuses wealth that would blur allegiance. He aligns with priestly authority that precedes national structure.

A person can engage in throne conflict without seeking a throne. Authority can be exercised without ambition. Victory does not require elevation.

The order of Melchizedek predates Israel's throne. It predates the law. It predates temple structure. It represents authority that flows from God Most High — not from territorial consolidation. Abraham aligns with that order. He does not create a rival throne. The conflict of thrones is not only about resisting counterfeit rule. It is also about refusing illegitimate elevation.

Abraham shows that you can defeat kings without becoming one. You can rescue without consolidating power. You can possess authority without seizing a throne. You can win battles and still remain under promise.

Abraham understood hierarchy. He knew where the throne was. He refused to blur allegiance for gain.

Abraham’s battle was not the final throne conflict. But it was a rehearsal. It demonstrated that authority flows from alignment. Victory does not require self-enthronement. The Throne belongs to God Most High. Every lesser ruler must answer upward.

THE THRONE THAT CANNOT BE SHAKEN

Before Creation, there was a Throne. Before rebellion, there was authority. Before conflict, there was rule. This book has traced the arc:

- The Eternal Throne.
- Created thrones.
- Usurpation.
- Counterfeit structures.
- The Wilderness refusal.
- The Cross and public exposure.
- Resurrection and enthronement.
- Delegated enforcement.
- The throne of the heart.
- Authority exercised without ambition.

Through every chapter, one truth has remained constant: Every conflict in Scripture is ultimately a conflict of thrones. It is a conflict of rule.

The throne was never vacant. Rebellion did not empty Heaven. Darkness did not dethrone God. The Cross did not repair a broken Throne; it revealed an unshaken one. The Eternal Throne was never contested in its origin. It was challenged in perception. Counterfeit thrones rose. Delegated authority fractured. Allegiance shifted, but the Throne itself remained.

Scripture declares:

> Yet once more I will shake not only the earth but also the heavens… so that what cannot be shaken may remain. (Hebrews 12:26)

Shaking does not threaten what is eternal. It exposes what is temporary. Counterfeit thrones tremble under scrutiny. Illegitimate crowns fall. Gates collapse. Altars are dismantled. What remains is what was never derivative, the Throne that cannot be shaken.

The final alignment history moves toward revelation. Not because God is striving. But because recognition will eventually match reality. Philippians 2:10 records:

> At the name of Jesus every knee should bow… and every tongue confess that Jesus Christ is Lord.

This is throne language. Knees bow. Tongues confess. Allegiance aligns. Not by force alone. By revelation.

The Eternal Throne stands. The resurrected King reigns. Delegated authority operates. Counterfeit structures weaken. The heart still chooses. The final question is not whether God rules. It is whether you will align.

Who occupies the inner seat?

What voice has final word?

What decree governs your fear, ambition, obedience, and worship?

A throne cannot remain empty. It is either surrendered to rightful authority — or occupied by something less.

Abraham refused self-enthronement. Jesus refused illicit initiation. The Cross exposed illegitimacy. The resurrection declared supremacy. The ascended King sits. They are seated. Permanently seated. This is the Throne that endures. From that seat, all history bends toward alignment. The Throne that was before Creation remains. Unthreatened. Unmoved. Unshaken.

Know this: Every other throne will eventually answer to it.

AFTERWORD

GOD SAID — & THEN A MAN SAID

God speaks first. He always has.

From the Beginning, authority entered history through decree: **"And God said, Let there be..."**

Light responded. Waters divided. Order formed. The pattern is consistent. God speaks. Reality aligns.

There is a pattern of interruption. Conflict enters when another voice follows. That voice is not always louder, not always hostile, but simply secondary.

In Genesis 3, God had already spoken. Then a voice said: "Did God really say…?" The issue was not information; it was authority.

Whose word would stand?

In 1 Kings 13, a man of God, a young prophet receives direct instruction. Clear. Specific. Unambiguous. Then an older prophet says, "I also am a prophet as you are…" The young prophet listens. He adjusts obedience to accommodate the secondary voice. The consequence is severe; the young prophet loses his life. God is not cruel, but authority cannot be outsourced. God had spoken. A older man spoke afterward. Jurisdiction shifted in a moment.

Did God not know the plans in the hearts of the king and the elder prophet before the young prophet ever got to that town? Yes He did. The words of the Lord to the younger prophet were to save his life, but he didn't obey. He wasn't rebellious; he was deceived perhaps by his own appetite or uncertainty. Or, both.

In the wilderness, the Father had declared:

"This is My beloved Son…"

Then the tempter said:

"If You are the Son of God…"

Jesus refused reinterpretation. He would not allow a secondary voice to redefine a primary decree. Alignment was preserved.

The question beneath the question. The issue is rarely whether God has spoken. The issue is what we allow to speak after Him. A parent may speak. A leader may speak. A culture may speak. A wound may speak. Fear may speak. Experience may speak, but none outranks the Eternal Throne.

Authority is revealed not by who speaks last, but by whose word is allowed to stand. This is where throne conflict becomes personal.

Every conflict of thrones eventually narrows to this: God said, then someone else said.

Which voice did you enthrone?

Which decree did you ratify?

Which word did you allow to govern?

Counterfeit thrones do not always overthrow through force. They reinterpret through suggestion. They dilute through familiarity. They reposition through credibility. But the pattern never changes.

God speaks. Then a voice follows.

HOW MANY HEAVENS ARE THERE?

Scripture uses the word "heaven" in at least three distinct ways. This is not three separate universes; it is three uses of the same term.

The First Heaven — The Sky / Atmospheric Realm. Genesis says, "God called the firmament Heaven." This refers to the visible sky, the atmosphere. This is where birds fly, and where clouds form. This is the lowest usage of the word, "heaven." It is physical.

The Second Heaven — The Celestial / Cosmic Realm. Scripture also refers to the sun, moon, and stars as being placed "in the heavens." This refers to the cosmic expanse --what we would call outer space was still created, and it is still physical.

The Third Heaven — The Dwelling Place of God.

I know a man in Christ who… was caught up to the third heaven. (2 Corinthians 12)

This is the only explicit numbering. The "third heaven" refers to the dwelling place of God. The

Throne room. The realm of Divine governance. The place of the Heavenly Court. This is not atmospheric, not astronomical. It is governmental. When Isaiah sees the Lord high and lifted up this is Throne-room Heaven. When Revelation describes the Throne standing in Heaven this is the Third Heaven.

Where are thrones in this hierarchy? The Eternal Throne is not "located" in the sky. It is described as being in the Highest Heaven, the dwelling place of God.

The heavens are the Lord's heavens, but the earth He has given to the children of men. (Psalm 115)

The Throne of God is consistently depicted as The Highest Heaven, the place of final decree. It is the seat of ultimate jurisdiction.

When Colossians speaks of "thrones, dominions, principalities, powers." These are created thrones. They may operate in heavenly realms, in the unseen realm. In what Paul calls "heavenly places." But they are not in the same category as the Eternal Throne.

"Heavenly Places"? Ephesians says Believers are seated with Christ in heavenly places. Also, that spiritual warfare occurs "in heavenly places. This suggests that "heavenly places" is a broader term than just the Third Heaven. It can include spiritual realms of influence, jurisdictional structures, and realms

where authority is exercised. Not all heavenly places are equal. Hierarchy remains.

Here's a very important clarification. The Bible does not teach a layered map such as Level 1 demons, Level 2 principalities, Level 3 throne room, Level 4 ultra-heaven. Scripture keeps it simpler: there's the created realm (Earth, sky, cosmos), and there is the unseen spiritual realm.

The Throne of God is above all.

The Eternal Throne is in the highest Heaven. Created thrones operate within the unseen realm under delegation. Counterfeit thrones operate within the same created realm — but in rebellion. Earth remains under human delegated dominion. The heart remains the decisive local throne. The Eternal Throne transcends all layers. It is not "higher" only spatially; it is higher jurisdictionally.

The number of heavens matters less than the clarity of authority. The Bible is less concerned with cosmological stacking and more concerned with rightful rule. There is one uncreated Throne; all other thrones are created, delegated, or counterfeit.

Now there was a day when the sons of God came to present themselves before the Lord, and Satan also came among them. (Job 1:6)

This scene clearly depicts **a heavenly court**. The elements are present. The Lord seated in authority.

The "sons of God" are presenting themselves; Satan appears among them. There is discussion and judgment regarding Job. This strongly resembles a royal court scene.

Scripture does not explicitly say that Satan entered the "third heaven" in Job. The phrase "third heaven" appears in Second Epistle to the Corinthians 12:2, where Paul describes being caught up to it. Many interpreters understand the heavens like this:

1. First heaven – the sky/atmosphere
2. Second heaven – cosmic/spiritual realm
3. Third Heaven – God's dwelling place

The Bible does not explicitly map Job's scene onto that three-level model. What Job clearly shows is that Satan does not operate as an equal rival to God. Instead, he appears before God's authority. He must give account. He receives limitations on what he may do. God says:

"Behold, all that he has is in your hand; only do not lay a hand on his person."
(Job 1:12)

This demonstrates **absolute throne hierarchy**. God's Throne governs the entire proceeding.

The scene is judicial. The structure looks like a court session; the Sovereign Judge presides. Servants report their activity. accusations are raised. permission is granted or denied. Satan functions almost like an accuser within the court. the word "*satan*," means adversary or accuser.

In Revelations 12, Satan is described as "the accuser of our brothers… who accuses them day and night before our God."

That passage also describes him being cast down. Some interpret this as indicating that his access to the Heavenly Court changes after Christ's victory. Christ Himself says in the Gospel of Luke 10:18: "I saw Satan fall like lightning from Heaven."

Job shows something very important about throne order: Even hostile spiritual beings operate under the authority of God's Throne. They cannot act independently, bypass Divine authority, or overturn the Throne. They must appear before it. This is why I said earlier, do not rail against dignities because they would not exist except that God allows it.

The Bible consistently presents a structure where God's Throne as the Heavenly Court, convenes and spiritual beings discuss Earthly events. Even Satan's actions occur within limits set by the Throne of God. The Throne of God is the ultimate governing authority of the universe.

No other power — earthly or spiritual — operates outside its jurisdiction. Even opposition must answer to that Throne.

GOD DOES NOT VACATE THE ETERNAL THRONE

The Lord is in His holy temple; the Lord's throne is in heaven. (Psalm 11:4)

The Lord has established His throne in the heavens, and His kingdom rules over all. (Psalm 103:19)

The Eternal Throne is not mobile in the sense of relocation. God is not spatially confined. He is Omnipresent. If He "moves," it is not because He was absent elsewhere. So, when Scripture describes Him *riding*, it is not describing Divine travel like a king changing palaces. Riding language is a theophany, which means that God is making His Presence and power known in a particular situation in some type of manifestation. Riding language is symbolic of God manifesting His authority, not of Him moving from place to place since He is already Omnipresent.

He rode upon a cherub and flew… (Psalms 18)

Ezekiel 1 describes wheels and living creatures beneath a Throne — this is theophany. Theophany is visible manifestation of Divine *Presence.* It communicates immediacy, intervention, judicial arrival, and manifest authority.

It does not mean that God vacated Heaven. It means He made His rule visible in a specific moment.

Manifestation vs. Location.

The Eternal Throne is the seat of ultimate Sovereignty; it is the center of jurisdiction. The mobile throne imagery shows the enforcement of Sovereignty within Creation.

The Supreme Court remains seated. But its rulings are enforced across the nation. Enforcement does not require relocation of the Court. It does not require relocation of sovereignty. The "riding" imagery shows enforcement entering history, not sovereignty relocating.

Does God "arise" for Judgment? Psalm language often says, "Arise, O Lord..." This is covenantal language. It does not mean God was inactive or asleep.

It means, Lord, manifest Your authority in this situation. When He rides in the imagery Judgment is being enacted. Covenant intervention is occurring. Authority is being revealed visibly, it is manifestation, not movement in space.

The Throne remains central. Even in Revelation, where the Lamb moves, opens seals, and acts. The Throne remains central. Heaven is not described as emptied. Authority does not shift. The throne is stable. Action proceeds from it.

If someone thinks God leaves Heaven to ride elsewhere, they may unconsciously imagine multiple sovereign seats, or fluctuating jurisdiction.

The Eternal Throne is fixed in supremacy. The riding imagery reveals enforcement of that supremacy within time and space. When Scripture depicts God riding upon cherubim, it is not describing relocation of the Eternal Throne. It is describing the visible enforcement of its authority within Creation.

One Sovereign Throne. Manifest authority. No duplication. No vacating.

SEATED AT THE RIGHT HAND

If God's Throne is eternal and fixed… what exactly happened at the Ascension? Did Jesus *move* to Heaven? Did He *sit down* somewhere new? Was there an empty chair before?

"Sit at My Right Hand."

The Lord said to my Lord: Sit at My right hand until I make Your enemies Your footstool. (Psalm 110:1)

This is quoted repeatedly in the New Testament. After the resurrection, Christ ascends and is described as, "Seated at the right hand of the Father."

This is enthronement language. The Right Hand is authority language. In ancient royal courts. The right hand signified shared authority. Executive rule. Delegated governance, and co-regency. To sit at the right hand does not mean the Father moved over. It means that the Son's mediatorial reign is publicly installed. The Eternal Throne did not change occupants. The incarnate Son, having completed redemption, is now declared enthroned in visible authority as the God-Man.

That is new in redemptive history, not new in Divine essence.

What Changed at the Ascension? Not God's sovereignty. What changed was the public vindication of the Son. The installation of the resurrected Christ as ruling Messiah. The visible union of Divine and human authority. Before incarnation the Son is eternally Divine. After Resurrection the God-Man is enthroned as mediator. That is the redemptive shift.

Did Heaven gain a Throne? No. There was always one Eternal Throne. But now Revelation can say "The throne of God and of the Lamb." This is not two thrones fused. It is one Sovereign Throne now revealed as occupied in shared Divine authority by Father and Son. The Lamb is not seated on a secondary folding chair. He shares the Sovereign seat.

If we misunderstand the Ascension, we might think that God's Throne was incomplete before. Christ had to travel upward to gain authority. Heaven rearranged furniture. None of that is Biblical. Authority was always His by nature. The Ascension is public enthronement of the victorious Messiah, not relocation of Divine Sovereignty.

The seated Christ is made clear in Hebrews:

After making purification for sins, He sat down…

Sitting indicates completion, stability, finished work, established rule. A king who sits is not scrambling. He is reigning.

The Throne remains singular. One Eternal Throne. The Father and Son share Sovereign authority. The Spirit proceeds in Divine action. Created thrones remain subordinate. Courtroom scenes remain functional. Hierarchy is intact. Christ's supremacy is intact.

THRONES: Not A Game

Scripture treats authority as something sacred, structured, and dangerous when mishandled. Kings fall over it. Angels fall over it. Nations rise and collapse around it. Yet in the end, the story resolves with one simple declaration:

> The kingdom of the world has become the kingdom of our Lord and of His Christ, and He shall reign forever and ever. (Revelation 11:15)

AMEN

Dear Reader:

Thank you for acquiring and reading this book. I pray it has been an eye opener and will help you look at thrones in a new and theologically correct way.

In Jesus' Name, Amen.

Dr. Marlene Miles

I seal this book, all words, decrees, declarations and prayers herein across every realm, age, era, dimension, and timeline, past present and future and to infinity. I seal them with the Blood of Jesus and the Holy Spirit of Promise.

Let every retaliation against this word, these prayers, these decrees and declarations spoken, prayed, or said by the speaker, or heard by the listener, or anyone praying these words backfire without Mercy, to infinity against the evil perpetrator, in the Name of Jesus. **Amen.**

Christ of God (*The*) 3-book series

Christ of God, (*The*) Box Set, includes all three books

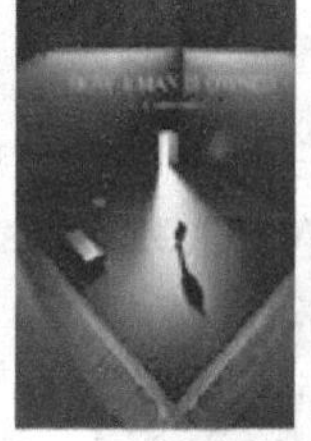

Prayerbooks by this author

While most books by this author have prayer points either throughout the book or at the end, there are some books that are only prayers. You just open up the book and pray.

Prayers Against Barrenness: ***For Success in Business and Life***

Fruit of the Womb: ***Prayers Against Barrenness***

Beauty Curses, ***Warfare Prayers Against***
https://a.co/d/5Xlc20M

Courts of Marriage: Prayers for Marriage in the Courts of Heaven ***(prayerbook)*** https://a.co/d/cNAdgAq

Courtroom Warfare @ Midnight ***(prayerbook)***
https://a.co/d/5fc7Qdp

Demonic Cobwebs ***(prayerbook)*** https://a.co/d/fp9Oa2H

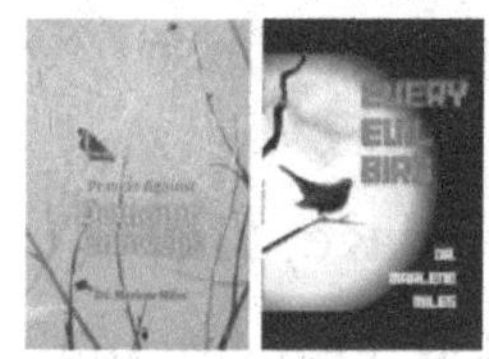

Every Evil Bird https://a.co/d/hF1kh1O

Gates of Thanksgiving

Spirits of Death, Hell & the Grave, Pass Over Me and My House

Throne of Grace: Courtroom Prayer

Warfare Prayer Against Poverty https://a.co/d/bZ611Yu

Other books by this author

AK: The Adventures of the Agape Kid

Already Married in the Spirit: *Why You May Not Be Married in the Natural*

AMONG SOME THIEVES https://a.co/d/dkYT4ZV

Ancestral Powers

Anti-Marriage, *The Spirit of*

Backstabbers https://a.co/d/gi8iBxf

Barrenness, *Prayers Against*
https://a.co/d/feUltIs

Battlefield of Marriage, *The*

Beware of the Dog: Prayers Against Dogs in the Dream.

Bless Your Food: *Let the Dining Table be Undefiled*

Blindsided: *Has the Old Man Bewitched You?*
https://a.co/d/5O2fLLR

Break Free from Collective Captivity

Broken Spirits & Dry Bones

By Means of a Whorish Father

Casting Down Imaginations

Churchzilla, The Wanna-Be, Supposed-to-be Bride of Christ

Demonic Cobwebs (prayerbook)

Demonic Time Bombs

Demons Hate Questions

Devil Loves Trauma, *The*

Devil Weapons: Unforgiveness, Bitterness,…

The Devourers: Thieves of Darkness 2

Do Not Swear by the Moon

Don't Refuse Me, Lord (4 book series)

https://a.co/d/idP34LG

Dream Defilement

The Emptiers: *Thieves of Darkness, 1*
https://a.co/d/5I4n5mc

Evil Touch

Failed Assignment

Fantasy Spirit Spouse https://a.co/d/hW7oYbX

FAT Demons (The): *Breaking Demonic Curses*
https://a.co/d/4kP8wV1

The Fold (5-book series)

- The Fold (Book 1)
- Name Your Seed (Book 2)
- The Poor Attitudes of Money (3)
- Do Not Orphan Your Seed (4)
- For the Sake of the Gospel (5)
- My Sowing Journal

Gang Ups: Touch Not God's Anointed

Getting Rid of Evil Spiritual Food

https://a.co/d/i2L3WYQ

got HEALING? Verses for Life

got LOVE? Verses for Life

got HOPE? Verses for Life

got money? https://a.co/d/g2av41N

Here Come the Horns: *Skilled to Destroy*
https://a.co/d/cZiNnkP

Hidden Sins: Hidden Iniquity

https://a.co/d/4Mth0wa

How to Dental Assist

How to Dental Assist2: Be Productive, Not Wasteful

How to STOP Being a Blind Witch or Warlock

I Take It Back

Legacy

Let Me Have A Dollar's Worth
https://a.co/d/h8F8XgE

Level the Playing Field

Living for the NOW of God

Lose My Location https://a.co/d/crD6mV9

Love Breaks Your Heart

Made Perfect In Love

Mammon https://a.co/d/29yhMG7

Man Safari, *The*

Marriage Ed. Rules of Engagement & Marriage

Made Perfect in Love

Money Hunters: Beware of Those

Money on the Altar https://a.co/d/4EqJ2Nr

Mulberry Tree, *The* https://a.co/d/9nR9rRb

Motherboard (The) - *Soul Prosperity Series*

Name Your Seed

Occupy: *Until I Return* https://a.co/d/bZ7ztUy

Plantation Souls

Players Gonna Play

Portals: Shut the Front Door: Prayers to Close Evil Portals.

Power Money: Nine Times the Tithe

https://a.co/d/gRt41gy

The Power to Get Wealth
https://a.co/d/e4ub4Ov

Powers Above

The Robe, Part 1, The Lessons of Joseph

The Robe, Part II, The Lessons of Joseph

Seasons of Grief

Seasons of Waiting

Seasons of War

Second Marriage, Third--, *Any Marriage*

https://a.co/d/6m6GN4N

Seducing Spirits: Idolatry & Whoredoms

https://a.co/d/4Jq4WEs

Shut the Front Door: *Prayers to Close Portals*
https://a.co/d/cH4TWJj

Sift You Like Wheat

Six Men Short: What Has Happened to all the Men?

Soul Prosperity soul prosperity series 3

https://a.co/d/5p8YvCN

Souls Captivity soul prosperity series 2

The Spirit of Anti-Marriage

The Spirit of Poverty https://a.co/d/abV2o2e

Spiritual Thieves https://a.co/d/eqPPz33

StarStruck- Triangular Power series.

SUNBLOCK- Triangular Power series.

The Swallowers: *Thieves of Darkness*, 3

Take It Back

This Is NOT That: How to Keep Demons from Coming at You

Thrones: It's Not A Game

Time Is of the Essence

Too Many Wives: *Why You Have Lady Problems*

Tormenting Spirits https://a.co/d/dAogEJf

Toxic Souls

Triangular Power *(series)*

- Powers Above
- SUNBLOCK
- Do Not Swear by the Moon
- STARSTRUCK

Unbreak My Heart: *Don't Let Me Die*

Uncontested Doom

Unguarded Hours, *The*

Unseen Life, *The* (forthcoming)

Upgrade: How to Get Out of Survival Mode

- Toxic Souls (Book 2 of series)
- Legacy (Book 3 of series)

The Wasters: *Thieves of Darkness*, Bk 2
https://a.co/d/bUvI9Jo

What Have You to Declare? What Do You Have With You from Where You've Been?

When I Was A Child, *I Prayed As a Child*

When the Devourer is Rebuked

https://a.co/d/1HVv8oq

The Wilderness Romance *(series)* This series is about conducting a Godly relationship and marriage with someone who is a Wilderness person. It is about how to recognize it and navigate through it. These books are about how not to get caught up in such.

- ***The Social Wilderness***
- ***The Sexual Wilderness***
- ***The Spiritual Wilderness***

Other Series

The Fold (a series on Godly finances) https://a.co/d/4hz3unj

Soul Prosperity Series https://a.co/d/bz2M42q

Spirit Spouse books

https://a.co/d/9VehDSo

https://a.co/d/97sKOwm

Battlefield of Marriage, The

https://a.co/d/eUDzizO

Players Gonna Play

https://a.co/d/2hzGw3N

Sent **Spirit Spouse (can someone send you a spirit spouse? This book is not yet released.)**

Matters of the Heart

Made Perfect in Love https://a.co/d/7OMQW3O

Love Breaks Your Heart https://a.co/d/4KvuQLZ

Unbreak My Heart https://a.co/d/84ceZ6M

Broken Spirits & Dry Bones https://a.co/d/e6iedNP

Thieves of Darkness series

The Emptiers https://a.co/d/heio0dO

The Wasters https://a.co/d/5TG1iNQ

The Swallowers https://a.co/d/1jWhM6G

The Devourers: Why We Can't Have Nice Things https://a.co/d/87Tejbf

Spiritual Thieves

Triangular Powers https://a.co/d/aUCjAWC

Upgrade (series) ***How to Get Out of Survival Mode*** https://a.co/d/aTERhXO

www.ingramcontent.com/pod-product-compliance
Lightning Source LLC
LaVergne TN
LVHW030921080826
845145LV00013B/3003

* 9 7 8 1 9 7 1 9 3 3 3 6 8 *